The Jumbo
Book of
Card Tricks
& Games

The Jumbo Book of Card Tricks & Games

Sheila Anne Barry, Bob Longe,
William A. Moss & Alfred
Sheinwold

Sterling Publishing Co., Inc.
New York

Library of Congress Cataloging-in-Publication Data

10   9   8   7   6   5   4   3

Published by Sterling Publishing Company, Inc.
387 Park Avenue South, New York, N.Y. 10016
© 2001 by Sterling Publishing Company
Material in this book previously appeared in *World's Best Card Tricks,*
© 1991 by Bob Longe; *101 Amazing Card Tricks,* © 1993 by Bob Longe;
Easy Card Tricks, © 1995 by Bob Longe; *Great Card Tricks,* © 1995 by
Bob Longe; *World's Greatest Card Tricks,* © 1996 by Bob Longe;
Mystifying Card Tricks, © 1997 by Bob Longe; *Card Tricks Galore,* © 1999
by Bob Longe; *World's Best Card Games for One,* © 1992 by Sheila Anne
Barry; *10-Minute Card Games,* © 1995 by William A. Moss; and *101 Best
Family Card Games,* © 1992 by Sterling Publishing Company
Distributed in Canada by Sterling Publishing
% Canadian Manda Group, One Atlantic Avenue, Suite 105
Toronto, Ontario, Canada M6K 3E7
Distributed in Great Britain and Europe by Chris Lloyd at Orca Book
Services, Stanley House, Fleets Lane, Poole BH15 3AJ, England.
Distributed in Australia by Capricorn Link (Australia) Pty. Ltd.
P.O. Box 704, Windsor, NSW 2756 Australia

Sterling ISBN 0-8069-6681-5

CONTENTS

CARD TRICKS

A FEW HUNDRED WORDS
OF ADVICE

It's hard to believe, but quite a few magicians do tricks for their own entertainment. If a spectator also happens to enjoy them, fine. But that's only incidental to the wonder the magician feels at his own superb ability. There's nothing wrong with this.

Some magicians prefer to show tricks only to other magicians, hoping to fool them with skill or a new principle. There is nothing wrong with this, either.

Both types of performer are missing the real fun of magic in which the marvel, wonder, and mystery of the trick are shared with an appreciative audience. The magician should not lord it over the group, but should be equally surprised. In effect, the magician is saying, "We're enjoying this together, and I'm just as excited about it as you are."

Don't misunderstand me. I occasionally show my tricks to other magicians. It can be fun and challenging. But you're unlikely to fool fellow magicians, and it's even less likely that they'll admit it if you do. A typical appreciative comment would be, "Very nice." If completely fooled, a magician might say, "Show that one to Joe," hoping, of course, to figure it out when you repeat the trick.

You should listen to and learn from fellow magicians, but be selective. Don't forget that some magicians have a fairly narrow view. For instance, I've heard some magicians complain, "There are too many four-ace tricks." What they really mean is that they have seen too many four-ace tricks. The average person has probably never seen a four-ace trick. Clearly, you can learn a lot from your fellow magicians, but try to remember that your primary audience consists of people who do not perform magic tricks.

You may have performed a trick a hundred times, but this audience has never seen it before. Don't be jaded. Try to bring the same enthusiasm to the trick as you had the first time you performed it. But with more skill, of course.

So, experiment, practice, and enjoy. We should all be performing for the fun of it, even when we're being paid.

TIPS

Practice

There are many right ways to perform a card trick. Unfortunately, there are also many wrong ways. You must know the trick inside out; the mechanics of it should be almost automatic.

After you've practiced on your own, it's time to victimize those close to you—your spouse, your siblings, your intimate friends. You'll discover whether a trick works for you without risking embarrassment before a less friendly audience.

Don't Tell What You're Going to Do

If you announce what you're going to do, you eliminate the element of surprise, but there's even a worse possibility. When you say, "I am going to cause these two cards to change places," spectators are watching for it and stand a better chance of catching you. Occasionally, a trick's effectiveness will depend on your announcing your intention, but this is the exception.

The Effect Is Everything

There's no particular relationship between a trick's difficulty and its effect. Many card artists believe that the more sleights they perform, the better the trick. Actually, the number of sleights is irrelevant. As a performer, you must try to view the trick as the audience does. What does the audience see? Two cards change places. Does it matter that you used three sleights? If you use one sleight or no sleights, the two cards still change places.

The standard for any trick should be: "Does it deceive, impress, and entertain the audience?"

Tell a Story

Good patter will not only entertain, it will also lead the audience in the wrong direction.

For each trick, then, I recommend that you create some kind of story. You can say that certain cards have an affinity for one another, or that the chosen card is quite obstinate and doesn't like to do what the rest of the cards do, or that this effect has never worked for you before but that the law of averages should operate in your favor this time.

Don't memorize patter. Instead, have a pretty fair idea of what you want to say and, when you practice, say it in a variety of ways. Memorized patter sounds stilted.

SLEIGHTS

These are the sleights needed to perform certain of the tricks. They can also be used for countless other tricks, perhaps some of your own invention. These sleights are relatively easy, and, when done properly, undetectable. The expert card performer should master a variety of sleights.

Double-Cut

This is a complete cut of the deck. Suppose you wish to bring a card to the top. Spread the deck for the return of a selected card. The spectator sticks the card into the deck. As you close up the deck, slightly lift the cards above the chosen card with the fingers of your right hand. This will enable you to secure a break with your little finger above the chosen card (Illus. a). (If the card is to be brought to the bottom, secure a break *below* the selected card.)

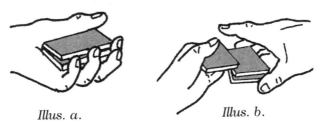

Illus. a.   *Illus. b.*

Holding the deck from above in your right hand, transfer the break to your right thumb. With your left hand take some of the cards from the bottom and place them on top (Illus. b). Take the remainder of the cards below the break and place them on top. (It is perhaps more deceptive if you move three small packets from below the break instead of two.)

This is, by far, the most common way in which magicians control a card to the top or bottom.

As you will see, this is also a sleight which has many other uses in certain tricks.

DOUBLE-LIFT

The double-lift is used in many tricks. A proficient card handler should definitely know how to do one. There are at least a dozen different ways of performing a good double-lift. The three below work extremely well.

Snap Double-Lift

Apparently a card is casually snapped face up and flipped back on top of the deck. Actually, it's two cards.

First, you should practice the display of a single card by snapping it face up. Incidentally, if you want to make the double-lift believable, always display a card in the same way as you do when performing the sleight.

Hold the deck high in your left hand (Illus. a). Your right hand lifts off the top card, holding it as shown in Illus. b. Squeeze the card so that it bevels downward, as shown in Illus. c. The idea now is to press down slightly with the first finger and continue bending the card, until by straightening the second finger slightly you snap the card loose from that finger and hold the card between your thumb and first finger (Illus. d). At the same time as you snap the card, turn your hand clockwise so that the card is clearly displayed. The entire move is done in an instant.

The card is returned to the deck by laying its side on the tips of your left-hand fingers, and flipping it over with your right-hand first finger (Illus. e).

Practice the entire maneuver until you can do it smoothly and naturally.

For the double-left, you duplicate precisely the actions in the single-lift. Holding the deck high in your hand, casually rif-

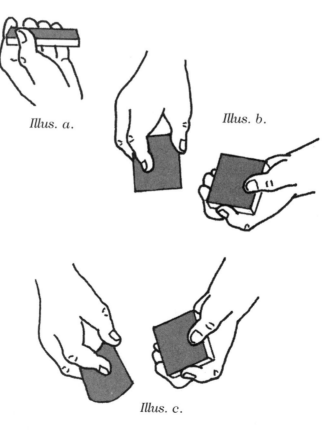

Illus. a.

Illus. b.

Illus. c.

fle the left side of the deck near the rear with your right thumb (Illus. f). In doing this, separate the top two cards from the rest of the deck and hold the break with your left thumb (Illus. g).

Take the two cards with your right hand exactly as you took the single card. Snap the two cards face up. Name the card. Roll the two back on top. Do all this in precisely the same way as you did the single card.

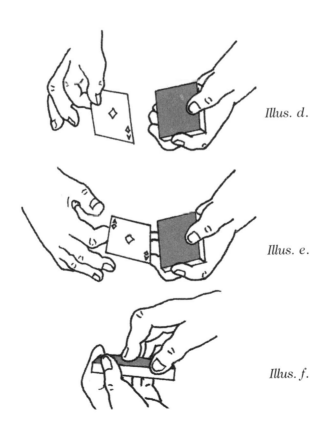

Illus. d.

Illus. e.

Illus. f.

Illus. g.

There's a knack. At first, the cards may separate slightly, but if you treat the two precisely as you would a single card, they won't. Alternate snapping over a single card and a double card. Within half an hour, you should have the move mastered.

Note: I was told that this was one of John Scarne's favorite methods. I don't know whether he invented it.

Efficient Double-Lift

I developed this double-lift some time ago. Since then, I've seen other magicians use double-lifts that are similar, if not identical. I believe that the details make this one of the best: It looks natural, it requires no preparatory move, and the return to the deck is extremely simple.

Hold the deck in your left hand, thumb along the left side. With your right hand, grip the deck from above, thumb at the rear, first finger folded on top, and the remaining fingers at the outer end (Illus. a).

Bevel the cards back slightly. With your right thumb, lift two cards about a quarter of an inch. The backward bevel helps with this. Slide your fingers back along the surface of the double card so that you're gripping it at the back end between fingers

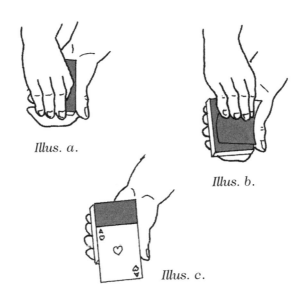

Illus. a.

Illus. b.

Illus. c.

and thumb (Illus. b). Immediately snap the double card over end-for-end, moving your right hand forward as you do so. Set the card down so that it projects about an inch and a half beyond the front of the deck (Illus. c).

After pausing a few moments, with your palm up right-hand grasp the double card at the right outer side, fingers below and thumb on top (Illus. d). Lift it off the deck and bring it to the right side of the deck (Illus. e). With your right fingers beneath, flip the double card face down on top of the deck.

It may be difficult at first to separate two cards from the deck with your right thumb. A good way to practice is to perform the double-lift, then deal the top card down. Perform another double-lift; deal the top card down. Continue on through the deck. Eventually, you'll have no trouble at all.

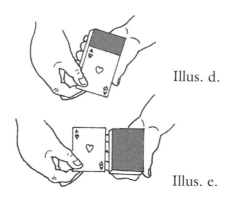

Illus. d.

Illus. e.

Original Double-Lift

The double-lift I learned as a kid is quite easy and will still do the job for a great many tricks.

As with *Efficient Double-Lift*, hold the deck in your left hand with your thumb along the side. Grip the deck with your right hand, as in the previous double-lift (Illus. a, page 17). As you chat with the spectators, separate two cards at the rear of the deck with your right thumb. Push these two cards forward about a quarter of an inch.

With your right hand, grasp the two cards at the outer end, finger beneath and thumb on top. This is precisely the same grip shown in Illus. d, except that, in this instance, the card taken with your right hand is face down. Turn the two cards over end-for-end, and set them down so that they project about an inch beyond the front of the deck.

When ready, grasp the cards at the outer end again, turn them end-for-end, and return them, face down, to the top of the deck.

TRICKS WITH THE DOUBLE-LIFT

Sneaky Slide

Have a card chosen and bring it to the top of the deck. (See *Double-Cut*, page 15.) Double-lift the top two, showing the wrong card. Turn the double card face down on top. "There you are, five of clubs," you declare. But the spectator says that you're wrong. You replay: "Oh-oh! I guess I'll have to try real magic."

Take the top card off the deck, grasping its outer edge with your right hand. Pass it through the middle of the deck, from the front end to the back . Turn the card over, showing that it has magically changed to the chosen one.

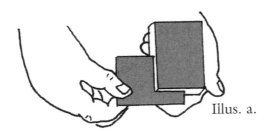

Illus. a.

My Mistake

Have Elizabeth choose a card and show it around. When she returns it to the deck, bring it to second from the top. Simply obtain a little-finger break *one card above* the chosen card after it's returned. Then perform a double-cut (see *Double-Cut*, page 15).

Explain to the group, "I know you're going to be astonished by this effect, but please hold your applause. When I reveal the chosen card, just marvel in silence so that we all can enjoy the enormous impact."

Perform a double-lift, showing the selected card. Name the card, and then say, "Oh, I'm sorry. I really don't miss that often. I have no idea what went wrong."

Return the double card to the top of the deck and slide the top card into the middle of the deck.

"Maybe I can work something out." Ask Elizabeth, "What was the name of your card?"

She tells you the name. All the spectators will be happy to inform you that you just stuck the chosen card into the middle of the deck.

"That's all right," you say. "After all, I *am* supposed to be a magician."

Tap the top card and turn it over.

That's Right, You're Wrong!

I developed an improved handling of a trick called "Righting a Wrong," which appeared in Jean Hugard and Fred Braue's *The Royal Road to Card Magic*.

Ask Barney to choose a card. When he returns it, bring it to the top. (See *Double-Cut*, page 15.) "Barney," you say, "please think of any number from 5 to 15."

Hand him the deck and ask him to count off that number onto the table. Ask him to *look at* the last card dealt.

"Is that your card?" No. Have him replace the pile on top. "I don't like to criticize, but maybe you didn't count them exactly right."

Pick up the deck. Suppose his chosen number was 11. Deal off ten cards slowly and precisely. "The important thing is to deal the cards *slowly*. Now wouldn't it be amazing if I had your card right here? What was your card?"

Suppose Barney says, "Queen of spades." You double-lift the top two, showing, say, the ten of clubs. "Oh, no, the ten of clubs. I should have guessed. The ten of clubs is a real trouble-maker, always popping up when you least want it."

Turn the two face down, and deal the top card (the one chosen) face down onto the table to one side. "So we'll just eliminate that nasty ten of clubs." Place the dealt cards back on top of the deck, commenting, "The trouble is, I dealt the cards *too slowly*. If you deal the cards too slowly, this will never work."

Count off ten cards onto the table, saying, "*Now* it should work." Show the top card. It's the ten of clubs. "Ten of clubs again! Wait a minute...what was your card again?" Turn over the card on the table. "That's it!" Act disgusted. "Just what I thought. The ten of clubs ruined everything."

Am I Blue?

A bit of preparation is necessary. For purposes of patter, you must use a red-backed deck. Note the bottom card of the deck. From a blue-backed deck, take a duplicate of that card and place it on the bottom of the red-backed deck.

The situation as you begin: You have, say, a king of hearts second from the bottom of your red-backed deck. On the bottom, you have another king of hearts, which has a blue back.

Fan through the cards, asking Lois to choose one. (Make sure you do not get to the bottom and reveal the blue-backed card.) As she shows the card around, close up the fan. Perform the Hindu Shuffle, as follows. Start with the deck in the dealing position in your left hand. With your palm-down right hand, grasp the cards at the near narrow end. Bring the deck toward you with your right hand, allowing your left fingers to draw off a small packet from the top (Illus. a). This packet falls into your left hand. Draw off another packet, letting it fall onto the one in your left hand. Continue until only a small packet remains in your right hand. Drop this on top of the others.

Illus. a.

At about the middle of the deck, stop and ask Lois to replace her card. Hold out the cards in your left hand for the return.

Drop the card in your right hand on top. The blue-backed card is now above the chosen card.

"I wonder if you'd mind blowing on the deck." After she does so, say, "Blow a little harder, please." If this is evoking amusement, you might ask her to blow even harder. "Oh, my! I think you blew too hard." Fan through the deck to the blue-backed card. Cut at the point to bring the blue-backed card to the top. "You *really* blew. In fact, you turned one of the cards blue." Ask, "What was the card you chose?"

Lois tells you. Do the double-lift, demonstrating that the blue-backed card is, in fact, the one she selected. Turn the double card face down and deal the top card (blue-backed) onto the table.

At this point, you have a blue-backed king of hearts face down on the table and the duplicate of that card on the bottom of the deck.

"Let's try it again," you say. You'll now perform the Hindu Shuffle force as follows. You have your force card on the bottom of the deck. With your first move, you not only withdraw a packet from the top, but you also cling to a small packet on the bottom with your left thumb and left fingers. The packet from the top falls on top of this packet. Complete the shuffle in the usual way. Apparently you've performed a regular Hindu shuffle; actually, the bottom several cards remain exactly as they were. This means, of course, that the force card is still on the bottom. Perform this maneuver a few times.

"Tell me when to stop," you direct Lois. Then commence the Hindu Shuffle. When she says stop, show her the bottom card of those in your right hand. Replace these cards on top.

Repeat the business of having her blow on the deck. "Let's

see if it worked." Fan through the deck, but this time there's no blue-backed card. Close up the cards and have her blow on the deck again, but once more you fail to find a blue-backed card.

Look puzzled. "I think I know what happened. What's the name of your card?" She names it. "Just as I thought. The king of hearts is a troublemaker, and a really mixed-up card. It can't make up its mind whether it wants to be blue or red." Turn over the card on the table. "See what I mean?"

Pause for a moment. Pick up the blue-backed king of hearts and place it in your pocket, saying, "We'd better get rid of that little rascal."

Further thoughts

Perhaps you're wondering, "As I proceed with other tricks, won't people notice that the king of hearts is back in the deck?" They might, and if they comment, you say, "Oh, yes, that little rascal is back." On one occasion, a spectator said to me, "But you put the five of spades in your pocket." My reply was, "Oh, that was a different five of spades," and I went into the next trick.

Yes, it occasionally works well to tell spectators the truth. Since you're a magician, they're unlikely to believe you anyway.

Note: This clever trick was shown to me by Wally Wilson.

Stay Put!

Ask Lois to cut off about half of the deck. You hold half and she holds half. Say, "Please turn over your top card so we can see what you have." Suppose she turns over the eight of hearts. Say, "Ah, the eight of hearts. You know, the eight of hearts is considered good luck. So you have the eight of hearts. Turn it face down, please, and let's see what I have."

Note that you say the name of her card at least three times.

Double-lift to show your card, announce its name, and replace it face down on top of your packet. "Now we exchange cards," you say. She lifts off her card and places it face down on your packet, as you lift off your top card and place it face down onto her packet.

Snap your fingers. Double-lift, turning over the top two cards of your packet. Your card has returned. Turn the double card face down. Make sure that Lois does *not* turn over her card. Again she places her top card on your pile as you place yours on top of hers.

Snap your fingers. Your card has returned once more, with the aid of the double-lift. Repeat the procedure again. Once more, do a double-lift, showing that the card has returned.

To help you keep track, you perform *four* double-lifts.

After the last double-lift, turn the card face down, saying, "Keep yours, I'll just put mine on your pile." After you put your top card on her pile, say, "Put your hand on top of it so that it can't get away." Snap your fingers and turn over your *top card*. The card's back again!

Ask, "And your card was the eight of hearts, right?" She agrees. Have her turn over her top card. It's the eight of hearts.

Ambitious Ace

Openly fan through the deck, removing the ace, two, and three of hearts and placing them on top. It doesn't matter *how* you place them on top, but they must be (from the top down) in this order: ace, two, three.

Hold the cards face down in your left hand in the dealing position. Spread out the top several cards and obtain a break with your little finger beneath the fourth card from the top. With your right hand, turn over the top *three* cards sideways, letting them drop on top of the deck. Comment, "So here we have the ace, two, and three of hearts."

With your palm-down right hand, even up the cards and lift off the top four. "Here's the three," you say. Draw the card onto the deck with your left thumb, making sure it's jogged about a half-inch to the right. Bring the remaining cards in your right hand beneath the three of hearts and, with them, flip the three over onto the deck (see Illus. a). Show the two of hearts, saying, "Here's the two." Draw it off with your left thumb, and flip it over in the same manner. As soon as the two of hearts lands face down on the deck, drop the two cards remaining in your right hand on top of it. "And the ace," you say. Turn the ace face down.

Illus. a.

The top four cards now are: ace of hearts, any card, two of hearts, three of hearts.

You continue, "Let's see what happens with the ace of hearts." Take the ace of hearts face down in your right hand. Push off the top card a bit and slide the ace of hearts under it. Give the ends of the deck a little riffle. Double-lift the top two cards, showing that the ace has returned to the top. Turn the two cards face down. Lift off the top card and place it on the bottom.

Now you're done with sleight of hand; the other miracles occur automatically.

As you turn the ace of hearts face down, comment, "Just as I thought." These three cards are extremely ambitious. They always want to be on top. We'll get rid of the ace." At this point, place the top card on the bottom.

Now on top are the ace of hearts, two of hearts, and three of hearts. Say, "Let's see what happens with the two of hearts." Place the top card second from the top. Give the deck a little riffle. Turn over the top card, showing that the two of hearts has returned to the top. (Make sure you turn it over in exactly the same manner as you previously performed the double-lift.) "Yes, the two is also very ambitious." Turn the two of hearts face down, take it from the deck, and place it on the bottom.

Deal with the three of hearts exactly as you dealt with the two of hearts, placing it on the bottom after you turn it face down.

"Yes, the two of hearts and the three of hearts really like being on top. But the most ambitious of all is...the ace of hearts." Turn the top card over, showing that the ace of hearts has returned. Again, *make sure you turn it over exactly as you turned the cards over with the double-lift.*

Note: This is a Nick Trost version of an Al Baker trick.

DISCOVERY

Discovery is the theme of some of the most imaginative card tricks, yet the basic idea is one of the simplest. A card is chosen, and the magician locates it.

Do-It-Yourself Discovery

This is one of the first impromptu card tricks I ever tried. The spectators' response told me that I had just performed real card magic. I was elated and determined to continue astonishing and mystifying.

The spectator shuffles the cards. Tell him to take half and give you the rest. "Now," you say, "while I turn my back, pick out a card, look at it, show it to the rest of the folks, and put it back on top of your pile."

Turn away and secretly turn two cards face up in your pile: the bottom card and the second card from the top.

When the spectator indicates that he is done, turn back, and tell the spectator to hold out his cards. Place your pile on top of his, even up the cards, and then direct him to place his arm behind his back, saying, "Now I want you to perform a little experiment with the cards behind your back."

Make sure of two things: that no spectator can see what goes on behind your assistant's back and that the assistant does not bring the cards forward until you are ready. To accomplish the latter, hover over the spectator, keeping alert to any premature disclosure. If he starts bringing the cards in front, say, "No, no, not until the completion of the experiment."

The position of the deck now: A card is face up second from the top, and a card is face up above the spectator's card in the middle of the deck.

"Take the top card...no, put that one on the bottom, so you'll know I'm not trying to fool you. Have you done that? All right. Take the *next* card, turn it face up, and stick it in the middle. Even up the cards."

Now you have the spectator bring the cards forward. Take the deck and fan through until you come to the face-up card. Ask the spectator to name his chosen card. Turn over the next card. "As you can see, you have located your chosen card yourself."

Once in a great while, the spectator will stick the card between your face-up card and the chosen card. You still have a decent trick. When you turn up the wrong card, simply say, "Oh, my! You missed by one." Turn up the next card, showing that it is the selected one. When doing tricks like this, where you are trying to hide the presence of face-up cards, it is best to use a deck with a white border.

Ups and Downs

With this trick, a selected card is found at the precise point a spectator tells the magician to stop dealing.

For years, I tried to work out a good way to do this. There are plenty of ways, but most require advanced sleight of hand and look pretty fishy. One day a few years ago, I stumbled on a very simple method. It is not so simple, however, that it doesn't astonish spectators.

A chosen card must be brought to the top of the deck. A pro would use sleight of hand; we'll try subterfuge.

As I considered various sneaky methods, I recalled a device used in an old trick called *Card from the Pocket*. Combining a variation of this device with my new idea would produce a doubly astonishing trick. A spectator looks at a card at a chosen number down in the deck. The performer causes the card to move from that number to a spot in the deck chosen completely at random by the spectator. Best of all, the working is clean and there is no sleight of hand.

Turn your back and have the spectator shuffle the deck. Say, "I would like you to think of a number from five to twenty. Now count down to that number, taking one card under the other so that you don't reverse their order. Look at the card that lies at that number, show it around, and replace the cards on top."

Turn around and take the deck, saying, "We have a chosen card that lies at a freely selected number down in the deck. Now, quick as a flash, I'm going to move your card to a much more convenient spot."

Place the deck behind your back, move the top card to the bottom, give the ends a noisy riffle, and bring the deck forward. It should take no more than a few seconds.

"All set. But first, let's make sure I *have* moved your card. What number down in the deck was it?"

When he tells you, deal the cards into a pile, one on top of the other, until you get the chosen number. Deal that card out face up. As you place the dealt pile on top of the deck, say, "Not your card, right?"

Naturally, it is not. Pick up the card and stick it face down into the middle of the deck. The chosen card is now on top.

"I would like you to watch for your cards as I deal, but don't say anything if you see it." Deal the cards into a pile. The top card is face down, the second face up, the third face down, the fourth face up, and so on. After you have dealt ten or so, tell the spectator, "Please tell me when to stop."

When he says stop, offer to deal more if he wishes. If he chooses to have you deal more, go ahead. And at the next stop, again offer to deal more. It doesn't matter to you. Just remember to continue the face-down, face-up pattern.

When the spectator stops you, pick up the pile of cards and place them on top of the deck, apparently to straighten up the pile. But by no means comment on this. Fan quickly through the cards to the last face-up card and lift them off (including the last face-up card). Set the rest of the deck down with your left hand. The top card of the deck is, of course, the selected card. As you fan through the cards and lift them off, ask, "Do you see your card among these?" Of course he doesn't.

"Then let's take a look at the face-down ones." Deal the packet into a face-up pile. Face-down cards are turned over and dealt face up; others are simply added to the pile as they are. "Seen your card yet?" He hasn't.

"Are you sure you remember the name of your card?" When he assures you that he does, ask him the name. Nod knowingly and say, "Of course." Tap the top card of the deck and turn it over. "See? I told you I was going to move your card to a much more convenient spot."

Here's a minor point which could make all the difference: When you deal the cards into a face-down, face-up pile, make sure that they overlap enough to conceal that first face-down card, which, of course, is the chosen one.

Lucky Seven

Start by discussing how lucky the number seven is, and then ask a spectator to do a trick for you. Hand him a deck of cards and turn away.

Say, "Please shuffle the cards, and then count off seven and set the rest of the deck aside. Look at the top card and show it around." After he has done so, continue: "Think of any number from one to ten. Transfer that many from top to bottom, one card at a time."

Turn back, take the seven cards, and place them behind your back. Reverse their order by taking them one on top of the other into the right hand. Patter about having to hold the cards behind your back for exactly seven seconds to make the experiment work.

"Time's up," you declare, bringing the cards forward. Hand them to your assistant. Turn away again. Say, "Please transfer the same number from top to bottom. Turn back and tell the spectator to place the top card on the bottom, the next on the table, the next on the bottom, and so on. When he has one card left, stop him, saying, "What is your card?" He turns it over, and that's it!

The "Milking" Trick

Turn your back and ask a spectator to quietly deal two piles of cards with the same number in each pile. He can have, say, ten to twenty cards in each pile. "Set the rest of the deck aside," you say. "We won't be using it. Now look at the top card of one of the piles and remember it. Pick up the other pile. Take a smaller number of cards from that pile and place them on top of your chosen card. Hide the pile you're holding."

Turn around and pick up the packet containing the spectator's card. "We must give the packet a mystical double-card shuffle," you explain. Grip the cards from above with the left hand, thumb at the inner end, fingers at the outer end. Begin "milking" the cards into a single pile. That is, remove a card from the top and bottom at the same time with the thumb and fingers of the right hand and drop them into a pile (Illus. a). Continue until all the cards are dealt this way. If one card remains, place it on top.

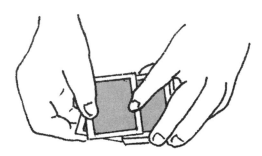

Illus. a. Remove a card from the top and bottom at the same time with the thumb and fingers of the right hand and drop them into a pile.

Pick up the pile and toss out the bottom and top cards face up. "Neither of these is your card, right?" You are right. Place both cards face down on top of the packet. You have managed to add an additional card to the top of the packet.

Point out that you have no way of knowing how many cards the spectator has concealed. Ask him to take these cards and deal them into a pile as you deal yours into a separate pile. You deal card-for-card from your packet as he deals his cards. When he deals his last card, turn over the card you are dealing. It is the chosen card.

Note: This is a modification of a trick invented by Alex Elmsley and revised by Stewart Judah.

Lucky Card Location

The spectator seems to make all the choices, yet you end up finding the chosen card. F. J. Baker had the original trick, which required a blank card. Since I seldom have one, I changed the handling slightly.

You must have a complete 52-card deck. Have Leonard shuffle the deck. Take the cards back, saying, "I have to find my lucky card. If all goes well, it will help with our next experiment." Fan through the cards with faces toward you. You must count to the 25th card. It will help allay spectator suspicion if you count the cards in groups of three. (Separate the card after you count off 25.) The 26th card from the bottom is on the face of the pile in your left hand (Illus. a).

"Here's my lucky card," you declare. Name the card. "If it's to do any good, we'll have to turn it over." Turn it over in

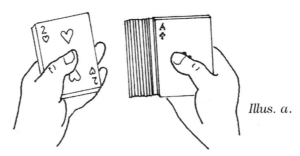

Illus. a.

place. Close up the cards. Turn the deck face down. The 26th card from the bottom is now face up in the face-down deck.

Hand the deck back to Leonard, saying, "Please think of a number from one to ten." Turn away. "Count off that number of cards from the top and place them in your pocket or hide them somewhere else. I don't want to know your number." Pause. "Now look at the card that lies at the same number from the top. Be sure to remember that card because now that's your lucky card."

Turn back to the group. "We have my lucky card turned face up somewhere in the deck. Now let's try my lucky number. I wanted a lucky number that no one else had, so I chose 13. Please deal off 13 cards into a pile." Leonard does so. "Now into another pile, deal as many cards as you want, but make sure you deal past my lucky card, or this trick won't work."

When Leonard finishes, pick up the second pile he dealt and turn it face up. "Take the other pile, Leonard. Let's deal our cards into separate piles. I'll deal mine face up; you deal yours face down. We'll do it together so we match each other card for card. When we come to my face-down card, stop the deal." Turn the card over, saying, "There it is…my lucky card." Ask him to name the card he chose. Point to the last card he dealt and ask him to turn it over. "Look at that; there's *your* lucky card."

Count Off

I came across this trick in a magic magazine, where it was referred to as an "old trick." I performed it for several months, and then I realized that I had invented the trick decades earlier. Over the years, however, someone had added a refinement that enhances the effect. Here's the new, improved version.

Have Lillian thoroughly shuffle the deck. Spread the cards out face up, showing how thoroughly the cards are mixed. Note the top and bottom cards. Add them together. Suppose the top card is a five and the bottom is a seven. The sum is 12. Turn the deck face down and start to spread the cards out, offering the choice of a card. As you do so, secretly count off 12 cards and hold these slightly separate from the rest (Illus. a).

Illus. a.

(The number you count off is the same as the total of the top and bottom cards. When you count off the cards, count in groups of three.) Make sure the card is chosen from below these. After Lillian looks at the card and shows it around, lift off the top 12 cards and extend the rest of the deck for her to replace the card. Place the 12 cards on top, even up the deck, and set the deck on the table. From this point on, don't touch the cards.

It's time for a bit of distraction. Address the spectators: "The deck was thoroughly shuffled by Lillian, who then freely selected a card. I haven't changed the position of a single card in the deck. Yet, if we're lucky, we'll see a miracle." Gesture toward the deck. "Lillian, please cut off a *large* chunk of cards." You want to make sure she cuts off well over half the deck. "Notice...complete freedom of choice." Point to the small packet, the former lower portion of the deck. "Please turn this pile face up." Call attention to the value of the bottom card of the pile. "Now pick up the other packet and deal into a pile that same number of cards."

Now have her turn the dealt pile face up. She notes the value of the bottom card and deals that many into a third pile. This pile is also turned up, the bottom card noted, and that many dealt into yet another pile.

"Enough piles, right? So what was the name of the chosen card?" After it's named, have Lillian turn the last pile face up. There's the chosen card.

I am always a little surprised at the conclusion. Three different cards are counted off from a shuffled deck, and the chosen card is found.

Further Thoughts
At the beginning, when you fan through to add the top and bottom cards, the total may be unusually high—20, for instance. When this occurs, have the cards reshuffled.

I Didn't Know

Here we have an extremely deceptive trick that is so much fun to do. Complete success depends on how good an actor you are.

You need to know the top card of the deck. But spectators must not suspect this. As you gather up cards from a previous trick, you might make sure you get a known card on top. Or, again while gathering cards up, you might notice the bottom card. Then earnestly discuss the previous trick with spectators as you perform a casual overhand shuffle. You shuffle the last few cards singly, thus bringing the bottom card to the top. Done properly, it should appear that you're merely finding something for your hands to do as you converse.

Set the cards down and ask Scott to assist you. He's the perfect choice, since he's anxious to please and will follow instructions exactly. "Scott, I'd like you to cut off a small packet of cards from the top of the deck—somewhere in the neighborhood of 10 to 20." Turn away. "Now please think of a number from 1 to 10. Do you have one? Good. Now move that number of cards from the top of your packet to the bottom, one by one. Do this very quietly. Let me know when you're done."

When Scott says he's done, turn back and take the packet from him. "Do you know how many cards are here, Scott?"

He does not.

"Let's find out." Count them aloud, either into your hand, taking one on top of the other, or onto the table; the important thing is that you reverse the order. Let's suppose the number is 12. "So, Scott, we have 12 cards here. And there's no way I could possibly know which one of these is your chosen card." Place roughly half the packet in each hand. "Now which one of these packets do you think contains your cards?" Put the packets back together so that they are in the same order as they were after you counted.

Somewhere along the line, Scott interrupts you to say something like, "But I don't *have* a card."

Here's where the acting ability comes in. "You didn't look at a card?" Pause. "Well, that's okay. You *did* think of a number though, right?" Right.

Hand Scott the packet. "When I turn away, move that number of cards from the top of your packet to the bottom, one by one." Turn away and provide these additional directions: "Now look at your bottom card and remember it." Pause. "Have you done that? Good. Let's see now...Have you shuffled the cards?" He hasn't. "Might as well give them a little shuffle."

This shuffle really throws everyone off—including magicians. In fact, you might as well have Scott give the cards *another* shuffle. At this point, you could read Scott's mind, since the card he looked at is the original top card which you peeked at. There's nothing wrong with doing this. A reasonably intelligent person will know, however, that you had some way of knowing the card in advance.

So, with a more sophisticated group, you might want to take the packet from Scott and go through the cards, studying them carefully. Finally, remove the chosen card (the original top card of the deck), and place it face down on the table. Scott names his card and then turns your choice over. Now when spectators wonder how you could have done it, they are faced with many more possibilities, and the real method is totally obscured. Just another one of your many miracles.

They Always Get Their Man

Fan through the deck and toss the red jacks face up onto the table.

Explain to the group, "You've probably heard stories of the valiant Canadian Mounted Police, or, as they are sometimes known, the Mounties. Who can tell me what they're best known for?"

Someone is bound to get the right answer: "They always get their man."

"That's right. And we're going to put that theory to the test. We'll see if the sterling qualities of the Mounties can be transferred to the playing cards which represent them."

Point to the face-up red jacks on the table.

"Here we have two Mounties. I'm sure you notice their traditional red jackets."

Rosemarie has always had an interest in officers of the law, so ask her to assist you.

Casually fan seven cards from the top of the deck. Lift them off and hand them to Rosemarie, saying, "Rosemarie, I'd like you to pick a criminal from those cards. You can either choose one from the underworld…" Indicate the bottom card of the packet: "…or you can choose one from the top echelons of crime."

Indicate the top card.

"So, when you're done shuffling, look at either the top or the bottom card. But don't do it just yet. After you've chosen a criminal, you'll perform a peculiar shuffle. Then I'll put one of the Mounties on top of the packet and one on the bottom, and you'll perform the same kind of shuffle again. But you don't have to remember all of that. We'll take it step by step. So, when you're ready, look at the top or bottom card."

If she looks at the *top* card, she performs an *under-down* shuffle: She places the top card on the bottom of the packet, the next card onto the table, the next card on the bottom, the next card on top of the one on the table, etc. When she is left with one card in her hand, she places this on top of those on the table.

You lead her through the shuffle, saying, "Put the top card on the bottom of the packet, deal the next card onto the table, put the next one on the bottom of the packet..."

If she looks at the *bottom* card, she performs a *down-under* shuffle. The first card goes onto the table, the next one on the bottom of the packet, the next onto the table, etc. And, as before, the last card she holds goes onto the pile on the table. Again, lead her through the shuffle.

"So now our criminal is buried somewhere in the packet. These two jacks are supposed to be Mounties, so let's see if they can behave like Mounties. The packet you're holding, Rosemarie, represents a big mountain with thousands of trees on it. The Mounties know that the criminal is somewhere on the mountain, so they're going to search it from top to bottom."

Hand her one of the red jacks face up. "Please put one Mountie on top of the packet face up." Hand her the other jack. "And put the other Mountie on the bottom of the packet face up."

When she finishes, hold out your left hand palm up. "Please place the packet onto my hand."

After she does, place your right hand on top and give the cards a quick shake. "This gets them started on their search." Lift up your right hand and have her take the packet back.

"Now, Rosemarie, you must take them on their search."

This time, she will *always* perform an under-down shuffle. "Put the top card on the bottom, deal the next card onto the table, put the next card on the bottom, deal the next card on top of the card on the table."

If necessary, take her through it the rest of the way. In all likelihood, however, she won't need any coaching after the first two cards.

Take the cards from the table. Fan them out. Fan down to the face-up red jacks. Between them is a face-down card. Remove all three together and set them onto the table. *Put the rest of the cards on top of the deck.*

"Well, the Mounties captured someone. Let's see how they did. Rosemarie, what's the name of the criminal you chose?"

After she names the card, you turn over the "captured" card.

"So the Mounties got their man. But how did those jacks *know* they were Mounties?

"And how did they find their man? Who knows? You know what I think? I think it's just coincidence."

At this point, you'll probably get some sarcastic comments from the group.

Further Thoughts

• *Putting the remainder of the packet back on top of the end of the trick is important. A spectator trying to reconstruct the trick will find it extremely difficult without knowing the correct number of cards. In fact, after the trick is over, a spectator will sometimes ask, "How many cards did you give me?" As usual, I lie, saying, "I don't know. I didn't notice." This clearly implies that the number is irrelevant.*

- *Early on, you tell your assistant that she'll perform a peculiar shuffle and that later she'll perform the same kind of shuffle. But even when she performs a down-under shuffle the first time, she must perform an under-down shuffle the second time. Does this make you an obvious liar? Not really. The shuffles are the "same kind"; they're just not identical. So far, no one has called me on there being a difference between the two. If anyone ever says to me, "Hey, those two shuffles are different," I'll reply, "Of course," and continue on.*

Note: This is my slight variation of a trick by Phil Goldstein. I changed the working a bit and the patter quite a bit.

Let's Play Jacks

In a "sandwich" trick, a chosen card is discovered between two significant cards, usually jacks. "Sandwich" tricks are always colorful and fun. This version by Al Leech is not only easy, but also extremely effective. I have revised the basic move slightly to make the trick even easier.

Take the red jacks from the deck and place them onto the table face up. Say, "The red jacks are real buddies. Generally, they like being together all the time. I'll try to prove that in a minute. But first, let's have Charles choose a card."

Charles selects a card. When he returns it to the deck, get a little-finger break above it. Bring it to the top of the deck, using *Double-Cut*, page 15.

Hold the deck in position to perform an overhand shuffle,

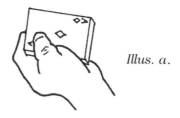

Illus. a.

but with the faces of the cards toward the left thumb (Illus. a). Ask Charles to pick up one of the jacks and turn it face down. "Charles, just drop it in here wherever you want. Just tell me when to stop."

Perform an overhand shuffle, taking several cards each time. The cards are landing in your left hand face up. When Charles tells you to stop, do so. Hold out the face-up cards that are in your left hand so that he can place his face-down jack on top.

Put the face-up cards that are in your right hand on top of all.

Turn the deck face down.

"We now have a face-up jack in the deck. I'll show you." Fan down to the face-up jack. Fan past a bit so that you can get a left little-finger break beneath the card below the jack. You're now holding a little-finger break below the chosen card.

Close up the cards and perform a double-cut, bringing the chosen card to the bottom of the deck.

Have Charles pick up the other red jack. "Turn the jack face up, please. Just tell me when to stop and drop it in."

Turn so that your left side is toward the group. You're about to perform another overhand shuffle, this time with the backs of the cards facing the left thumb, and you want to make sure that no one can see the bottom (chosen) card. As you shuffle this time, the cards land face down in the left hand. Charles tells you when to stop and drops the jack *face up* onto the face-down cards in your left hand. You drop the cards that are in your right hand on top of all.

The sneaky part is done.

"I promised that I could bring the red jacks together," you say, which is not quite true. "Let's see how I did."

Fan through the cards until you come to the red jacks with a card in between. "Whoops! What's this?" Take the three from

Illus. b.

the deck as a group. Make sure they are spread out, so that all can see them clearly as you display them (Illus. b). Put the three cards onto the table, still spread out. Set the rest of the deck aside.

Turn to the spectator who selected a card. "It looks as though someone's trying to break up their friendship. What was the name of the card you selected?"

He names the card. You turn over the usurper. Sure enough, that's the card.

Magic Is My Business

This is one of those rare puzzlers in which the deck is never handled by the magician.

Hand Beatrice the deck and turn your back.

Provide these instructions, with appropriate pauses: "Please shuffle the deck, Beatrice. Now just *think* of any card. Fan through the deck and find that card. Remove it from the deck and place it face up onto the table."

When she's ready, continue: "Let's say that you're to spell out the name of a card, using one card for each letter in the spelling. No one could possibly know how many cards are on the table. After all, the queen of diamonds has many more letters than, say, the two of clubs. So please pick up the deck and spell out the name of your card, dealing one card into a pile for each letter in the name."

Give her a chance to finish, then: "When you're done, put the rest of the deck aside. We're only going to use the cards you spelled out onto the table and your chosen card. So please turn your chosen card face down and place it on top of those you spelled out onto the table."

Turn back and face Beatrice, assuming, of course, that she hasn't absconded with your brand-new deck of cards.

"In a moment, Beatrice, I'll want you to spell out a sentence. You'll spell out, 'Magic business is magic.' Or you can spell out 'My magic is business.' Or perhaps, 'Business is *my* magic.' Or maybe you'd prefer a philosophical sentence like, 'Is magic my business?' Or even, 'Is business my magic?' Or you can even make an exclamation, like, 'My! Business *is* magic.' You have complete freedom of choice...any one of these sentences."

She chooses one of these—or any other 17-letter sentence. You help her as she spells it out, moving one card from the top to the bottom for every letter.

"I don't know how that helps us find your card, but it sure is fun, isn't it? Please hold out the packet."

Rest your hand on the packet for a moment and perhaps murmur an incantation, like, "This better work or I'm sunk." (This provides a reason for the trick to work. Unbeknownst to one and all, you—you slick one—*could have* done something sneaky while your hand rested on the cards.)

"Beatrice, you strike me as a very magical person. Maybe you can find your own card...with the cards face down. Let's try. Just deal the top card onto the table. Put the next card on the bottom of the deck. Put the next card onto the table, and the next on the bottom of the deck." Have her continue until she holds only one card. Don't let her turn the card over just yet. "There's no way in the world that I could find your card; let's see how you did."

She did perfectly.

"You know what, Beatrice? I think magic *is* your business."

Further Thoughts

If a spectator could remember exactly what you did, he could do the trick himself. But the steps are sufficiently complicated to make this unlikely.

Note: The basic principle used in this trick was developed, I believe, by Alex Elmsley. As far as I know, my use of the principle is unique.

PREDICTION

Presto Prediction

Few tricks have a climax as startling as this one. The principle is just about impossible to detect, but what really makes the trick work is the patter, the romance. I have always felt that a weakness can be turned into a strength if you only give the problem enough thought. In this instance, the spectators are dealing cards, selecting, counting down. In other words, this has all the earmarks of a "mathematical" trick, a no-brainer, a trick anyone could do. Indeed it is. But the patter makes it all seem logical, if not absolutely necessary. So at the climax of the trick, be sure to try the suggested patter.

Hand the deck back, holding it with your fingertips, so that all can see that you are doing nothing tricky. "Watch carefully. I want you to see that I do not change the position of a single card. I'm going to fan through the deck and remove a prediction card."

Demonstrate by fanning through the cards, faces toward you, noting the value of the top card. Close up the cards. Let us suppose that the top card is an eight.

"Watch carefully now!" With the cards facing you, again fan

through them, starting at the bottom. Since you noted an eight on top, count to eight from the bottom and note the card at that position. Let us say it is the five of diamonds. Continue fanning until you come to the corresponding card in color and value—in this instance, the five of hearts. Meticulously lift the five of hearts from the deck and place it face down on the table, stating, "This is my prediction card." While doing all this, handle the cards openly to emphasize that you are doing *nothing tricky* with the deck.

Hand the deck to the second spectator. "Please turn the deck face up and deal the cards one at a time into a pile." Once he deals past the card you noted, casually say, "You can stop whenever you want." When he does stop, tell him he may deal a few more, take a few back, whatever he wishes.

Take the undealt cards from the spectator and place them face down. Turn the dealt cards face down. The position now is as follows: The top card of the undealt pile indicates the number down in the dealt pile at which the match for your prediction card lies. In our example, the top card of one pile is an eight, and the eighth card down in the other pile is the five of diamonds, which corresponds to your prediction card, the five of hearts.

Point out the two face-down piles to a third spectator. "Perhaps you have seen demonstrations where the performer asks you to choose a pile and then he takes whatever pile he wants. In this case, I want you to pick up a pile. That will be the pile that you will actually use."

Sound convincing? Of course. But, as you will see, it doesn't matter which pile he picks up. Suppose he takes the pile with the eight on top. You say, "What we are going to do is turn over the top card of your pile—not yet—and count down that number in this pile." Pick up the other pile and continue, "An ace has a value of one, a jack eleven, a queen twelve, and a king thirteen." This statement is particularly effective when the card is *not* one of these, for it creates the impression that you have no idea of what the card is.

The third spectator turns over the top card of his pile; you slowly count off the cards from your pile, setting aside the card arrived at. In our example, the spectator turned over an eight, so you count off eight cards, setting aside the eighth one, the five of diamonds.

Suppose that when you offer the choice of piles the third spectator picks up the pile containing the card that matches your prediction card. Simply say, "Now I will turn over the top card of my pile, and we will count over the top of my pile, and we will count down that number in the pile you have chosen." Be sure to mention the business about the value of ace, jack, queen, and king. Let the spectator count off the cards, and you take the final card of the count and place it face down on the table.

You now have two face-down cards on the table: your prediction card and the card "chosen" by the spectators. Gather up the rest of the deck, leaving the two face-down cards.

What you say now triples the trick's effectiveness. "Let's review. First, the deck was thoroughly shuffled. Without changing the position of a single card, I removed the prediction card. Then you (the second spectator) dealt off as many cards as you wanted, stopped whenever you wanted. Finally, you (the third spectator) chose a pile, and we actually used the pile you chose. In other words, we tried to arrive at the choice of a card completely by chance. Why did we go through all this? Because if I offered you the choice of a card, you might think I had some way of forcing my selection on you. Instead, we have guaranteed that a card was chosen at random."

Set aside the deck. Take the two cards at the outer edge. "If I have correctly predicted the future, those two cards should match each other in color—and in value." Face the two cards simultaneously. When you gather the cards up after enjoying everyone's astonishment, it's fun to add, "I feel sorry for the next fifty-one people I do this for."

Further Thoughts
Occasionally, when fanning through the cards for your prediction card, you will see that it is among those that will be counted off. Obviously, the trick will not work. Shake your head, close up the cards, and hand them to a spectator, saying, "Please shuffle them again. I can't seem to picture a card; the vibrations just aren't right. Perhaps another shuffle will help."

Note: This trick appeared almost 40 years ago in a booklet I published. The trick was recently credited to someone else. I don't invent so many good tricks that I can afford to let that pass: I invented it, and besides, my version is better.

Colorful Prediction

With this trick, by using an unprepared deck you apparently correctly estimate the number of red and black cards in two piles.

For this one, you need a complete deck of fifty-two cards. Let a spectator shuffle the deck. Take it back and begin dealing into a face-down pile. After you have dealt fifteen or more, invite the spectator to tell you to stop whenever he wishes.

As you deal, count the cards. Try to keep your lips from moving. When he says stop, give him the dealt pile. Ask him his favorite color, red or black. Suppose he says red, and further suppose that his pile contains twenty-three cards. You say, "Bad luck. I have three more red cards than you have black."

Repeat the assertion. Now deal your cards face up, counting the red cards aloud as you go. The spectator deals his cards face up, counting the blacks. Sure enough, you have three more reds than he has blacks.

Why?

To understand, take a deck of cards, shuffle it, and deal it into two piles of twenty-six cards each. Suppose you have nineteen black cards in one pile. You must also have seven red cards in that pile. This means that the other pile must contain nineteen red cards and seven black cards. So, no matter how you shuffle, when you have two piles of twenty-six cards, you will always have the same number of black cards in one pile as you have red cards in the other.

This will be clearer if we take an extreme example or two. If you have twenty-six black cards in one pile, you will have twenty-six red cards in the other. You could say, "I have the same number of reds in my pile as you have blacks in yours."

It would work the same if you had twenty-five red cards and one black in your pile. The spectator would have twenty-five blacks and one red. And you, naturally, would have the same number of red cards as he has blacks.

If you tried to pass that off as a trick, however, very few spectators would be deceived, particularly if you do repeats. Therefore, you disguise the principle by working with unequal piles and performing a simple calculation.

When you performed the trick as above, the spectator had twenty-three cards. That's three less than twenty-six. You, therefore, have three more than twenty-six. This means that you have three more red cards than he has black. For that matter, you have three more black cards than he has red.

Back to the trick. The spectator is astonished at your clairvoyance, but you have only just begun. Have the spectator shuffle his packet of twenty-three, and you shuffle your packet. You may even exchange packets and shuffle. Then you take your original packet and begin dealing onto his, asking him again to tell you when to stop. Once more you keep track of the number.

He had twenty-three, so you begin counting with twenty-four. When he tells you to stop, you again know the number of cards he has in his pile.

"Which do you want this time, red or black?" Suppose he chooses black, and that he now has thirty cards in his pile.

"Good selection. You now hold four more blacks than I have reds."

In other words, he has four more cards than twenty-six.

You may repeat the trick a number of times, remembering to deal from the larger packet to the smaller. In our example, the piles would be shuffled again, and you would make sure to deal from the pile of thirty onto the other, which, of course, contains twenty-two.

The trick, like many good ones, is a combination of a hidden principle and verbal chicanery. You can throw spectators off further by stating your prediction in different ways.

There are four ways you could state the preceding prediction:

1. You now hold four more blacks than I have reds.
2. You now have four more reds than I have blacks.
3. I now have four fewer blacks than you have reds.
4. I now have four fewer reds than you have blacks.

Count On It

Have the deck shuffled. Take the deck back and prepare to fan through the cards, faces toward you. Note the bottom card. You're going to arrange for that card to become the 21st from the top. At the same time, you're going to find a card of the same color and value as that card, take it out of the deck, and place it face down as your prediction card.

Suppose the bottom card is the ten of diamonds. You will be hunting for the ten of hearts. Say, "I'll have to find a prediction card," as you begin fanning through the cards and counting them. When you have fanned out nine or ten, pause, shake your head, and place the group on top. Continue fanning and counting, picking up at the next number. When you reach 21, shake your head, and place that group on top. The 21st card from the top is now the ten of diamonds.

Continue fanning to the ten of hearts, take it from the deck, and place it face down on the table. Suppose, however, that the ten of hearts turns up in that first 21 cards. Pull it from the deck, studying it carefully. No, it won't do. Place it well above the middle of the deck. Continue your count from the point where you pulled the ten of hearts. After you arrange for the ten of diamonds to be 21st from the top, continue fanning to the ten of hearts. This time, take it from the deck and place it face down on the table.

Get a volunteer and say to him, "You are about to select a card. If I have correctly foretold the future, it should match my prediction in color and value."

Have the volunteer cut off a small packet of cards. He must take fewer than 21 cards. You now deal off 20 cards face up from right to left, overlapping so that the values can be seen.

"You don't know how many cards you have cut off, right?" Of course not. "It could be *any* number. Please count them." Turn your head aside while he does so.

When he's finished, tell him to start at his right and count that many over in the row on the table. He is to pull out the card he lands on.

Turn over your prediction card. Right again!

Corresponding Cards

After shuffling the cards, turn them with the faces toward yourself. Say, "I have to find a suitable prediction card. This is very difficult." Puzzle over the card as you fan through the deck.

Actually you note the bottom card. Counting it as one, you count through the face-up cards until you get to 13. Cut that thirteenth card to the top. Thus, the card you noted becomes the thirteenth card from the top of the deck. Continue fanning through the deck until you come to the mate of that original bottom card—the card that matches it in color and value. When you find it, remove it from the deck and place it on the table, saying, "There it is—my prediction card."

Suppose the mate to the bottom card is among the 13 you're counting from the bottom. No problem. Simply start counting to 13 from *the mate*. As before, cut when you get to 13. In this instance, the mate to the *original bottom card* will now be thirteenth from the top. Fan through until you get to the original bottom card. Place this face down on the table as your prediction card. It is, of course, the mate to the thirteenth card from the top.

Set the deck down.

Evelyn will help out. Say, "Evelyn, I'd like you to think of any small number, say 1 to 10. Now you'll have to remember that number. Then, while my back is turned, deal off that many from the top of the deck and hide them." Turn away from the group.

When she finishes, turn back. Take the deck, saying, "Now I'm going to take 12 cards." Count 12 cards into a pile on the table. Pick up the pile and place it behind your back. (If sitting at a table, you can take the cards under the table.)

"Evelyn, I'll bring out the cards one by one. When I bring out the card at your number, tell me to stop."

Behind your back, take off the top card, bring it to the front, and set it face down on the table. Continue with the next top card. Keep on going until Evelyn tells you to stop.

Bring forth the rest of the cards from behind your back and set them aside. The card at which Evelyn stopped you goes face down next to the prediction card.

"If I've correctly predicted the future, these two cards should match."

Turn over the two, showing that they're mates.

Note: Floyd Shotts invented this trick.

You Might Wonder

You might wonder why a trick this simple would work. After the deck is shuffled by a spectator, take the cards back. Comment that you need a prediction card as you fan through the deck, faces toward yourself. At first, fan rapidly through the cards, noting the top card. Then fan through more slowly, looking for the mate to the top card—the one that matches it in color and value. Remove that card and set it aside, face down, announcing that it's your prediction.

Hand the deck face down to Ernie, saying, "Please deal the cards one at a time into a face-down pile." After he's dealt 15 cards or so, say, "You may stop any time you wish." When he stops, take the remainder of the cards from him and set them aside.

Tell him, "Pick up the pile you dealt and turn it *face up*. Now deal those into a face-up pile and stop whenever you wish." Again, when he stops, take the cards remaining in his hand and set them aside. Say, "Pick up the pile, turn it face down, and deal as many as you wish."

He stops; you take the remaining cards and set them aside. He continues, alternately dealing from a face-up packet and a face-down packet, until only one card remains. Take this card and set it next to your prediction card. If the card is face up, simply turn over your prediction card, showing the match. If the card is face down, turn over the two cards simultaneously.

Further Thoughts

Make sure that the top card isn't an obvious one, like an ace or face card. On every other deal, the "chosen" card is briefly displayed, so it should be a spot card, which is unlikely to be noted. If the top card is an ace or face card, have a spectator give the cards an additional shuffle.

Mystic Prediction

Have Don shuffle the deck. Take it back, saying, "I'll attempt to predict the future, so I'll need to find a card that will match one that you'll choose by chance."

Fan through the cards, faces toward yourself. Explain: "Notice that I don't change the position of any cards as I look for a good prediction." Note the *eighth* card from the bottom. Find its mate in the deck—that is, the card that matches it in value and color. For instance, if the eighth card from the bottom were the queen of clubs, you'd find the queen of spades. Remove this mate and place it face down on the table. Announce, "This is my prediction card." If the mate should be one of the first seven cards from the face of the deck, have the cards reshuffled. "No card stands out in my mind; maybe you should give them another shuffle," you say.

Hand the pack to Don. "We're going to have you choose a card using a random mathematical procedure. I'll describe the method that seems to work best for this experiment. Deal the top card of the deck face up, saying 'Ten' aloud. Then deal the next card face up on top of it, saying 'Nine.' Continue down to one, or until you hit a match. Suppose you hit a six when you say 'Six' aloud. That would be a match, so you'd stop dealing in the pile. Then you'd begin another pile, again starting with ten. If you should get all the way down to one without a match, then you 'kill' that pile by placing a face-down card on top of it. In your counting, an ace is considered a one. And only tens count as ten; face cards don't.

"Undoubtedly you've heard that three, seven, and thirteen are mystic numbers. True enough. But for precognition, *four* is the critical number. So we'll need exactly four piles."

Guide Don through the process. Each time he hits a match as he counts backwards from ten, have him stop and start a new pile. If he deals out ten cards without a match, have him place a card face down on the pile, "killing" it.

After he has dealt four piles, gather up the "dead" piles, turning over the top card of each so that all the cards face the same way. Have Don shuffle this packet of "dead" piles. He places the entire packet beneath the pile from which he's been dealing.

Don adds up the cards on the face of the remaining packets. For example, if two packets remain, and the last cards dealt on these packets were 9 and 7, you'd get 16. "You have 16. Please deal 16 cards into a face-down pile."

Take the last card he deals and, without looking at it, place it face down next to your prediction card. "Let's see if my prediction worked out. If it did, these two cards should match in value and color." Turn over the two simultaneously.

Further Thoughts

- *This trick is actually enhanced by a repetition or two.*
- *In the unlikely event that all four piles are "dead," simply gather up all the cards and start the trick over.*
- *As mentioned, after the spectator has dealt four piles, gather up the "dead" piles, righting the top card of each. The spectator shuffles these together and places the stack on the bottom of the cards he has left. The reason: If you don't do this, a repetition will reveal that the chosen card is always eighth from the bottom.*

Note: This is a Martin Gardner principle with a Henry Christ twist. This is my variation.

Eliminate the Negative

June agrees to assist you, so ask her to give the deck a good shuffle. You take the cards back, saying, "Now I need to make a prediction." Fan through the cards, faces toward yourself. Note the top and bottom cards. Based on these two cards, you will select *two* cards as your prediction. One card will match the *top* card in value and the bottom card in suit. The other will match the *bottom* card in value and the top card in suit. Suppose the nine of clubs is on top and the queen of hearts is on the bottom. You will remove from the deck these two cards: the nine of hearts and the queen of clubs.

Set the two cards aside face down, saying, "These are my prediction cards. If all goes well, they will correctly predict our chosen card."

At this point, if you wish, you can give the deck a riffle shuffle. Just make sure you do not change the position of the top and bottom cards.

"June, we're now going to choose a card together. In the process, we'll discover whether our minds are on the same wavelength. To start, please cut the deck into two piles."

Let her create the two piles. Then, place your right hand over one pile and your left hand over the other. "Which one shall we eliminate?"

Now she chooses one of the piles, and you place it to the side. If she chose the original top portion of the deck, you know that you must keep track of the *bottom card* of the other portion. If she chose the bottom portion, then you must keep track of the top card of the other portion. In other words, you keep track of the original top card or the original bottom card, depending on which pile was discarded. We'll call this card the *key card*.

"June, would you cut the remaining cards into two piles and hold your hands above them the way that I did." She does so. "Now I'll choose a pile to eliminate."

Obviously, you choose the pile that does not contain the key card. Have her set this pile aside with the other discarded pile.

"To speed things up, how about dealing the remaining cards into five piles. Deal them out just as though you were dealing hands in a card game."

Again, keep track of the key card.

"Now I'll hold my hands over two piles, and you choose the one to eliminate." Naturally, you hold your hands over two piles other than the one containing the key card. June sets aside the pile you choose.

Four piles remain. June holds her hands over two of these. You choose a pile other than the one containing the key card. This pile is discarded.

Three piles remain. You hold your hands over the two that do not contain the key card. June chooses one, and it is set aside.

Two piles remain. June holds her hands over them. You choose the one that does not contain the key card, and that pile is discarded.

Remaining is one small pile. "Let's see what card we chose between us." The key card is either on top or on the bottom of this last pile. So, to display the key card, you either turn the pile face up or turn over the top card of the pile. In either instance, you announce the name of the card. "Ah, the queen of hearts!" you might say.

Turn over one of the prediction cards to see whether it's the suit or the value card. Let's say the card you turn over is the queen of clubs. You say, "And here we have a card which foretold the value...a queen. And we also have a card which foretold the suit..." Turn over the other card. "...a heart. The queen of hearts!"

Further Thoughts

• *As you fan through the deck to see what the top and bottom cards are, you might find that they are of the same suit or value. Just say, "I don't think these cards are mixed enough," and have the deck reshuffled.*

• *Quite often when you have eliminated all but one pile, that pile will contain exactly three cards. You can deal these out in a row and continue the elimination. You hold your*

*hands over the two piles that do not contain the key card.
And then June holds her hands over the two remaining
piles, and you choose the one that does not contain the key
card.*

• *The principle used in this trick is well known among
magicians and has been used frequently in tricks with coins,
poker chips, and other small objects. Years ago, I invented a
version using cards. Until I came across this trick, I didn't
know of any other adaptation of the principle to cards.*

Note: Hugh Nightingale developed an extremely clever trick
that required a slight setup and a calculator. Using his basic
idea, I came up with this totally impromptu trick.

The Red One

Here we have a "packet trick." This means that you have a
small number of cards in an envelope or wallet. These may be
trick cards of some sort, or they may simply be cards that you
don't ordinarily find in a deck—six jokers and two aces, for
instance. The point is that you take these cards out and perform
a wondrous trick.

Your packet, in this instance, consists of six cards. You'll be
happy to know that these are not "trick cards" in any way. But
neither are they ordinary.

So you have six cards. Five are black-spot cards (clubs or
spades); one is a red-spot card (heart or diamond). One of the
black-spot cards has a red back; all the other cards have a blue
back.

Ultimately, the cards will be laid out as in Illus. a. A spectator will be forced to choose either the second card or third card from your left. In our example, the face-down five of diamonds (the only red-faced card) is second from the left, and the face-up two of spades (the only red-backed card) is third from the left. In either instance, you'll demonstrate that the card selected is the only one different from the rest.

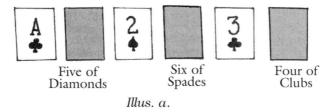

Five of
Diamonds

Six of
Spades

Four of
Clubs

Illus. a.

If the five of diamonds is chosen, you will turn over the other face-down cards. All the cards are now face up except the five of diamonds. You point out that all the other cards are black. Turn over the five of diamonds; it's the only red-backed card.

If the two of spades is chosen, you will turn over the other face-up cards. All the cards are now face down except the two of spades. You point out that all the other cards have blue backs. Turn over the two of spades; it's the only red-backed card.

Thus, it *appears* that the spectator chose the only card that's different from the others. Now let's see how precisely we arrive at this delightful conclusion.

Prior to your performance, set up the cards so that on top is the only red-faced card—in our example, the five of diamonds. Second from the bottom is the only red-backed card—in our example, the two of spades. (In our example, the setup from top to bottom will be five of diamonds, six of spades, four of clubs, three of clubs, two of spades, ace of clubs.)

In performance, get the assistance of Albert, who—poor boy!—actually thinks he has some degree of psychic ability.

"I'd like you to assist me in an experiment, Albert." Take the packet from your envelope, or wallet, or pocket. "I have six cards here. I'll send you a psychic message and see if you receive it."

Turn the packet face up and hold it in your left hand in the dealing position.

Illus. b.

In the illustration, the card at the face of the packet is the ace of clubs. Deal this card face up to your left. About four inches to the right of this, deal the next card (two of spades) face up. And, about four inches to the right of this, deal the next card (three of clubs) face up.

Illus. c.

Turn the remaining three-card packet over. You're now holding the packet face down in your left hand in the dealing position. Deal the top card (five of diamonds) face down into the first space on your left—in other words, between the face-up ace of clubs and two of spades. The next card (six of spades) goes face down into the next space to the right, between the two of spades and three of clubs. And the last card (four of clubs) goes face down on the right end. The cards are now in the position that was originally shown in Illus. a.

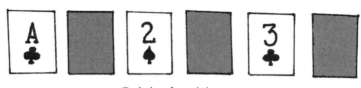

Original positions

"Six cards here, Albert, and I'm going to send you a psychic message." With fingers to temples, concentrate, hoping that Albert gets the message. "Now, Albert, please think of a number between one and six. After you've thought of one, change your mind, so that we'll know that this is not psychological. Do you have a number between one and six?"

He does. "Tell me the number, and we'll count it from the end."

Because you said "between one and six," he is confined to numbers two, three, four, and five. This means that Albert will end up with either the second or third card from your left. (Take a look at the original positions again, shown previously.)

If he gives the number two or five, he will end up with the second card from your left. Say he gives the number two. Start with the card on the left end and count one, two—ending on the second card from your left. If he gives the number five, start with the card on the right end and count two, three, four,

Illus. d.

five—again ending on the second card from your left. In either instance, push the "chosen" card forward about an inch or so (Illus. d).

Turn the other face-down cards face up (Illus. e). "Notice that all the others are black cards."

Illus. e.

Turn over the "chosen" card. "And you picked the only red card of the group. Albert, you really are psychic." Gather up the cards and put them away.

If Albert gives the number three or four, he will end up with the third card from your left. Suppose he gives the number three. Start with the card on the left end and count one, two, three—ending on the third card from your left. If he gives the number four, start with the card on the right end and count one, two, three, four—again ending on the third card from your left. In either instance, push the "chosen" card forward an inch or so (Illus. f).

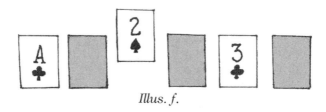

Illus. f.

Turn the other two face-up cards face down (Illus. g).

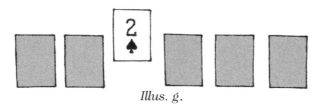

Illus. g.

"Notice that all the other cards have blue backs." Turn over the "chosen" card. "And you picked the only card in the group with a red back. Albert, you really are psychic."

Further Thoughts

• *It's easy to set up the cards so that you can perform immediately for another group. At the conclusion of the trick the six cards will either all be face up or face down. Simply gather them up so that the card that's second from the left becomes the top card (when the packet is face down) and the card that's third from the left becomes second from the bottom (also when the packet is face down).*

• *When you ask the spectator to choose a number between one and six, he might just choose one or six. If he does, say, "I said between one and six." Have him choose another number. It's your trick; you can make whatever rules you wish. When this occurs (which is very seldom), the trick loses a little, but is still effective.*

You might prefer this approach, however: Just spell O-N-E or S-I-X from the left. After all, if the spectator is not sharp enough to know what "between" means, he's probably forgotten that you said you'd count from the end, and he's probably also forgotten his middle name.

MENTAL

Either/Or Force

You must know the top card. Deal cards into a pile, telling a spectator to tell you when to stop. As soon as he says "Stop," start dealing another pile to the right of the first one. Again, the spectator tells you when to stop. Immediately, start dealing a third pile to the *left* of the first one. Once more the spectator tells you when to stop. Place the remaining cards in your hand to the far right.

Four piles are in a row on the table. You know the bottom card of the second pile from your left. Cover the two piles on the right with your outstretched right hand and the two piles on the left with your outstretched left hand. Ask, "Right or left?" Whichever is chosen, push aside the two piles on your right.

"Pick up a pile, please." If he picks up the pile containing the force card, push aside the remaining pile and tell him to look at the bottom card. If he picks up the other pile, take it from him and place it aside with the other discarded piles. Tell him, "Please look at the bottom card of your chosen pile."

This business is called the *equivoque* or the *magician's choice*, of which there are many versions. Try it out; it's quite easy and totally convincing.

Hopelessly Lost

There's apparently no way in the world a chosen card can be located. Yet you manage to find it.

Before you begin, peek at the top card and remember it; this is your key card. Fan the pack out face down and have Phyllis remove a group of cards from the middle. Set the rest of the deck down. Take the packet from Phyllis, saying, "I'd like you to *think* of one of these cards as I fan them out." Avert your head. "I won't watch your face." Of course you won't; you'll be too busy silently *counting* the cards as you slowly fan the faces of the cards for Phyllis's perusal.

After she's thought of one, hand her the packet. Turn away, saying, "Please remove your card and show it to everyone. Then place it face down on the table. Shuffle the rest of the packet and put that group on top of the deck. Now put your card on top."

You could continue giving directions with your back to the group. I usually find it best to turn back at this point to make sure my directions are followed exactly. Say, "Cut off about two-thirds of the deck, please. Set that group on the table. Take the remaining third and give those cards a good shuffle. Place them on top of the deck. Obviously, your card is hopelessly lost. Still, give the deck a complete cut."

The pack may be given additional complete cuts. Take the deck and turn it face up. Continue: "Let's see if I can pick up your mental vibrations. I'll fan through the deck and, when you see your card. I'd like you to think the word *stop*. I won't watch your face because I don't want to get any physical signals." What a nice person you are! Of course the main reason you won't watch her face is that you'll be looking for your key card. When you see it, begin silently counting with the *next* card.

Count the number that was in Phyllis's packet, and the last card you count is the one chosen.

Slow down as you near the end of the count, saying something like this: "I'm getting an exceptionally strong signal. Your card must be somewhere near. Perhaps I passed it. No! This is it, right here!"

What's on Your Mind?

This trick once more displays your ability to read minds.

Before you start, conceal three cards in your pocket, faces inward. Agatha probably knows how to shuffle, so give her a chance. Take the cards back and deal the top four cards onto the table. (Since you're going to memorize the cards, make sure you don't have two of the same value. Simply discard as unsuitable a card that matches another in value.)

"While I look away," you say, "I'd like you merely to *think* of one of these cards."

When she's done, gather up the cards, remembering their value from top to bottom. Suppose the cards are nine, jack, three, five. Simply repeat this to yourself several times.

Place the cards, face inward, into your pocket, on top of the three already there. Tell Agatha, "Please concentrate on your card."

Reach into your pocket and pull out one of the three cards you originally placed there. Don't let anyone see its face. After studying it for a moment, shake your head, and place it in the middle of the deck. Do the same with the other two cards you've previously placed in your pocket.

Return your hand to your pocket. Ask: "What was your card?" Separate the cards so you can quickly grasp whichever is named. Produce that card.

You might try a repeat; after all, you still have three cards in your pocket.

A Kingly Decision

Joe Hustler invented this extraordinarily effective trick. You must perform it to see what a strong result you get with a minimum amount of labor. A modest amount of preparation is necessary.

Remove from the deck the four kings. Place the king of clubs on top. The other three kings should be placed near the bottom. I generally put one on the bottom, one third from the bottom, and one fifth from the bottom.

Darla is excellent at shuffling the cards, so you should solicit her help. But first, you have some shuffling of your own to do. Give the deck two good riffle shuffles.

Hand the deck to Darla, saying, "Please give the cards a little overhand shuffle."

Once she takes the deck, pantomime the overhand shuffle motion. She should give the deck *only* one overhand shuffle. If she looks as though she might continue shuffling, place your hand on top of her hands and say, "I want you to listen carefully." This effectively stops her from giving the cards the extra shuffle that would spoil the trick.

Turn away from the group. "Darla, hold the deck so that the faces are toward you and no one else can see the faces of any of the cards. Now fan through and take out the first king that you come to. Hide that card somewhere. You can put it into a pocket, sit on it, whatever."

The first king that she comes to is the king of clubs.

"Next, take out the king that's the same color as the one you took. Please put that king in Herb's pocket." Obviously, you name one of the males who is present.

Turn back and face the group. Concentrate fiercely. At length point at Herb and declare, "The card in your pocket, Herb, is the king of spades. And, of course, Darla's king is the king of clubs."

The Force Is With You

Ask Stan to give the deck a shuffle. Take the cards back and say, "Stan, I could fan out the cards face up and ask you to think of a card, but you might feel that one card is more significant than the others. In other words, you might make a psychological choice." As you talk, hold the cards face up so that all can see the faces. Fan off a group of ten cards or so, saying, "You might think of one of these, for instance."

Place the group at the rear of the deck (on top if the deck is face down). Make sure you note the last card you fanned to, which is now the rearmost card (the top card if the deck is face down). You must remember this card. What's more, it must not be an obvious card, which the spectator might remember. The best choice would be a spot card. Let's say that the card you're remembering is the six of clubs.

You have just placed a packet to the rear of the face-up

deck. "Or you might think of one of these…" Fan out five cards and place them at the rear of the deck, just as you did the previous group. "…or one of these…" Fan out five more cards and place them at the rear. "…or one of these." Fan out a significant number of cards, lift them off the deck, and then replace them onto the face-up deck. Close up the deck and turn it face down. Say: "So you could look through the deck and think of a card, but some cards might stand out. In fact, you may have seen a card that stood out from the others. Let's avoid that."

Hand Stan the deck. "Instead, I'd like you to think of a number…say, from one to ten. Got one? Okay, now please change your mind. Again, we want to make sure you don't make a psychological choice." Pause. "I'll turn away, and I'd like you to deal that many cards onto the table…very quietly. Now hide them somewhere; put them into your pocket or stick them under something."

When Stan finishes, turn back and take the balance of the deck. Count off ten cards from the top of the deck, taking them one under the other. In other words, the cards should retain their order.

Turn the packet face up. "Stan, I'm going to go through these cards. Please remember the card that lies at the number you thought of." (The card at that number will be the card you're remembering—in our example, the six of clubs.)

"Here, I'll deal them into your hand." He holds one of his hands out, palm up. Make it very obvious that you're averting your head, so that you can't see the cards as you deal. Slowly deal the face-up pile one card at a time onto Stan's palm, counting aloud as you do so.

When you're done, take the cards from Stan and place them face down on top of the deck. Have Stan cut the deck.

Hold the deck to your forehead and gradually reveal the name of the card: "I see clouds, dark clouds. Your card is black...I'd say it's a club. Think of the value. I'm starting to get it...Yes, it's rounded...maybe a nine. No, no... *like* a nine...It's a six. Your card is the six of clubs."

Note: The brilliant Wally Wilson recently developed this wonderful force that works particularly well as a mental trick. I'm grateful that he recommended it.

COINCIDENCE

Crazy Coincidence

Fan through the deck, faces toward you. Make sure no one can see what you're actually doing. Pretending to contemplate, pick out eight red cards and place them in different spots, face down on the table. Pick out eight black cards and hand them to a volunteer to shuffle briefly. Take them back and place one, face down, on each of the cards on the table.

Ask the spectator to choose a pair. Pick the two cards up and turn them over. Holding one in each hand, name them, and say, "Please remember these two cards, which were freely chosen." Name them again. Reverse the order of the two cards when you bring them together, so that the former top card is now on the bottom. Place the two on the table with the other pairs.

Have your assistant gather up the pairs, placing them into one pile. He may collect them in any order. Now he cuts the pile three times.

"Please deal the cards alternately, making two piles." When he finishes, say, "Let's see what happened to the two selected cards." Name them again. Then turn over each of the piles. In one pile, all the cards are red except for the black selected card. In the other, all are black except for the red selected card.

Quadruple Coincidence

Preparation: On top of the deck you should have the ace, king, queen, jack, and ten of spades—a royal flush. They may be in any order, but the ten should be the third card down.

Start by riffle-shuffling the deck, keeping your stack on top. Now give the deck *one* overhand shuffle. Just pick up the bottom three quarters of the deck and shuffle these cards onto the top section. Your stack will be intact somewhere in the deck. Invite the spectators to give the deck a few complete cuts.

Say, "I'd like to demonstrate a simple fact: You can't beat the odds. If I place one card here on the table and someone chooses four cards at random, one of those cards will almost certainly match my choice. It's a matter of probability. So let's test it out."

Ask Steve to assist you. Tell him, "I'll choose a card—my prediction card. And I'll give you four chances to match it in value. I'm sure you can do it. In fact, I'd bet money on it, except that I'd be taking advantage of you."

Fan through the cards, faces toward yourself. Find the ten of spades. Cut the cards so that this becomes the top card, saying, "This is a perfect prediction card." Without letting anyone see it, take it from the deck and set it face down on the table.

The position: The ten of spades is face down on the table; two cards of the royal flush are on top of the deck and two are on the bottom.

Set the deck face down on the table and ask Steve to cut off a substantial portion. Take the cut-off cards from him and set them aside. Point to the bottom portion, saying, "Please deal those into two piles, alternating." When he finishes, the top card of each pile will be a card from the royal flush.

Point to the pile you set aside. "Cut off some of those, please." He cuts off a pile. Take the remainder and place them face down on top of your prediction card, saying, "We won't need these anymore, so we'll let them guard my prediction card."

Have Steve deal the cards he cut off into two more piles, alternating. When he finishes, the *bottom* card of each of these two piles will be a card from the royal flush.

"Let's give you even more choices," you say. Have him place the first two piles he dealt on top of the second two piles he dealt.

At this point, the top and bottom card of each of the two piles is a card from the royal flush. Have him pick up either pile. "Deal those into a pile and stop whenever you wish." When he stops, have him place the remaining cards on the table.

Have him pick up the other pile. He deals these into a pile, stopping when he wishes.

"Perfect! I'm sure that at least *one* of your choices will match my prediction card."

Turn over the pile that has your prediction card on the bottom, setting it on the table face up. "The ten of spades. Now let's see if we have a match."

Turn over one of the other piles so that it's face up on the table. Register disappointment, then say, "That's all right; I have three more chances."

Turn over another pile and react the same way. By this time, spectators are increasingly aware of what's happening. Turn over another pile and demonstrate considerable irritation. After you turn over the last pile, say sardonically, "Great! Not a single match!" Continue chatting as everyone else, of course, notices the royal flush. Make sure you leave enough time for all to notice it. Say, "I swear this works 99 percent of the time. I don't know what went wrong." Shrug and shake your head, displaying total dejection as you gather up the cards.

Further Thoughts

Clearly, if you prefer, you may have two spectators do the cutting and dealing, providing a bit more audience involvement.

The First Quadruple Coincidence

Phil doesn't believe in mentalism in any form, so he's the perfect assistant. Hand him the deck of cards and ask him to shuffle.

Take the deck back and hold it up so that the back of the deck is toward the spectators.

"I need a prediction card," you declare. Note the value of the bottom card.

Hold the deck face up so that all can see the cards. With your right hand, take the bottom card. Take the next card *on top of this.* Continue dealing cards, one on top of the other, until you've taken as many cards as you need to *spell out* the value of the bottom card.

For instance, suppose the bottom card is a three. As you take the cards, one on top of the other, into your right hand, spell to yourself, "T-H-R-E-E," taking one card for each letter. Place these five cards face down on the table to your right. So, on the table is a pile of five cards, the top card of which is the one you saw on the bottom of the deck, a three.

"Don't worry, I'll find a good prediction card." Again, start taking cards one on top of the other into your right hand until you come to a card that matches the original bottom card—in this instance, another three. The three, then, is the last card you take into your right hand. Turn the cards in your right hand face down and place the group on top of the pile on the table. In our example, you now have two threes together, fifth and sixth from the bottom of the face-down pile on the table.

"Need a prediction," you mumble. At this point, if you wish, you can stop taking the cards one on top of the other; instead, just fan rapidly through the cards until you come to another three. This three you cut to the *back* of the face-up cards you're holding. (In other words, the three would be the top card if the packet were face down.)

At this point, tilt the deck toward you so that spectators can't see the faces of the cards. Fan through to the fourth three. Without letting the group see its face, place this three face down well in front of you.

"At last, my prediction!"

Place the rest of the cards in your hand face down onto the pile on the table. In our example, a face-down three is set forward as your prediction card, the top card of the deck is a three, and the fifth and sixth cards from the bottom are threes.

Pick up the deck and turn it face up. Rapidly deal the cards into a face-up pile. After you've dealt 15 or so, say to Phil, "You can tell me to stop anytime."

When you're told to stop, pick up the pile you've dealt off, turn it face down, and set it down to your right. Place the packet remaining in your left hand face down to your left.

"You chose when to stop, Phil. Now please touch one of the piles. We'll use the one you choose."

Suppose he chooses the pile on your left. "All right," you say. Turn over the top card of the pile and replace it, face up, onto the pile. "So you chose a three. Let's spell that out." Pick up the other pile. Spell T-H-R-E-E aloud, dealing one card into a pile for each letter in the spelling.

If Phil should touch the pile on your right, say, "All right, we'll spell down in the pile you've chosen." As before, you turn over the top card of the pile on the left and spell out that value in the pile on your right.

In either instance, you touch the last card dealt out and say, "Wouldn't it be a coincidence if this turned out to be a three also?" Turn the card over, showing that it is a three, and place it face up on top of the others you dealt off. Place the remainder of the deck directly in front of you.

The cards on the table should now form a diamond pattern, as in Illus. a.

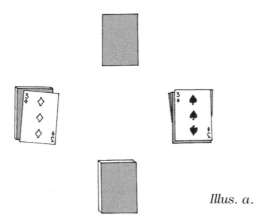

Illus. a.

"Wouldn't it be even more of a coincidence if my prediction card turned out to be a similar card?"

Turn over your prediction, showing it to be a three.

Touch the pile directly in front of you. "And what must this card be?" Turn it over to show that it also is a three.

Summary

1. *A spectator shuffles the deck. You take it back, saying, "I need a prediction card."*

2. *Hold the deck face up and note the value of the bottom card. Let's assume that it's a three. Silently spell out the value of this card, taking one card under the other for each letter. In this instance, spell out T-H-R-E-E. Place this pile face down onto the table.*

3. *Continue going through the deck, taking one card on top of the other, until you come to another three, which will be the last card you take into your right hand. Place this pile face down on top of the first pile.*

4. *Fan rapidly through the cards until you come to a third three. Cut the cards so that this three becomes the top card.*

5. *Tilt the deck toward you so that others can't see the cards. Fan through to the fourth three. Without letting anyone else see its face, place it face down well forward of you. "At last, my prediction!"*

6. *Place the rest of the cards in your hand face down on top of the pile on the table. Pick up the deck and turn it face up. Rapidly deal the cards into a face-up pile. After dealing 15 or so, ask a spectator to tell you when to stop.*

7. *When stopped, turn the dealt-off cards face down. Place the remaining cards in your hand face down to the left of this pile.*

8. *Ask a spectator to choose one of the piles. If he takes the one on your left, you turn over the top card of that pile and say, "So you chose a three. Let's spell that out." Pick up the other pile and spell T-H-R-E-E, dealing out one card for each letter in the spelling.*

9. *If the spectator chooses the pile on your right, say, "We'll spell down in the pile you've chosen." As before, turn over the top card of the pile on your left and spell out the value in the other pile.*

10. *Indicate that you're hoping for a coincidence as you turn over the last card you dealt out in the spelling. It is also a three. Turn it face up and place it on top of the cards you just dealt out.*

11. *Place the remainder of the deck directly in front of you. The cards should now form a diamond pattern.*

12. *Turn over your prediction card, showing that it's also a three.*

13. *Turn over the top card of the remainder of the deck; it's the fourth three.*

Further Thoughts

• *Once in a while this happens at the beginning of the trick: You note the bottom card and start to spell out its value, taking cards into your right hand. But one of these cards is of the same value as the bottom card. Obviously, the trick won't work. Give the deck a quick shuffle and start again.*

• *The placing of the four cards in a diamond formation is not only visually pleasing, but also provides a dramatic touch which enhances the trick considerably. It makes sense,*

therefore, to pause after the revelation of the fourth card,
letting all enjoy the configuration and the startling climax.

Note: A few years ago I invented a trick that I called
"Quadruple Coincidence." Soon after, I came across an older
trick of the same name, invented, I believe, by Frank Garcia.
Offhand, I can't think of a better impromptu trick. It dawned
on me a short while ago that a basic component of the trick is
a discovery of mine from many, many years ago.

Lucky Numbers

Beforehand, take the two red queens from the deck. Place one
on top of the deck and one on the bottom.

Jenny enjoys a good card trick, so she'll probably be happy to
help you out. Set the deck onto the table and say, "Jenny, would
you please cut off about half the cards and place them onto the
table next to the others?"

After she does this, pick up the original lower portion of the
deck, saying, "Let's see how close you came to half." Count the
cards aloud as you take them one on top of the other. (If you
prefer, you can count them into a pile on the table.) Whatever
number you end up with, say, "That's amazing. You just gave
them a casual cut, and you came extremely close to cutting
them exactly in half. Now I know this experiment is going to
work."

At this point a red queen is on top of each pile.

Place the piles side by side. "In magic, Jenny, there are two really significant numbers—seven and thirteen. We're going to use both of them in this experiment. Let's start with seven. Please give me any number from one to seven."

Suppose she chooses four. Counting aloud, you deal four cards simultaneously from each pile, placing each card face down next to its pile. In other words, you deal to the right of the pile on the right, and to the left of the pile on the left.

Turn over the top card of each of the piles you dealt off. Usually, the cards will be quite different in suit and value. Comment on their differences.

If their suits or colors happen to be the same, mention, "Good! That's a start."

If the cards happen to be of the same value, say, "This is amazing. Four must be your lucky number."

Turn the two cards face down and replace them on the dealt-off piles. Place the dealt-off piles back onto their original piles. "Now, Jenny, let's try the number 13. Please give me any number higher than seven but not more than thirteen."

Let's say she chooses 11. As before, deal off that number to the side of each pile. Again show the top card of each pile you dealt off. Comment on the cards, calling attention to their similarities and differences. Replace these cards face down on top of their respective counted-off piles. Place the counted-off piles back onto their original piles.

"So far," you say, "we haven't accomplished much. But let's see if your two chosen numbers have *combined* power. Your numbers were four and 11. So we'll start with four."

As before, you simultaneously deal the cards to the side of each packet. With the first card, you say, "Four." With the

next, you say, "Five." Continue until you deal the card num-
bered 11.

"Jenny, let's see if these cards in any way match." Turn them
over and hold them side by side. "Perfect! How symbolic! You
chose two beautiful ladies."

Further Thoughts

• *If you do the trick for a man, you might prefer to use
kings or jacks. At the end, you comment, "You chose two
handsome men."*

• *When dealing the cards simultaneously, you might find
it easier to pick the cards off from the rear, fingers on top
and thumb below.*

Note: This is my version of a Peter Wilker trick in which he used
an old principle to fashion an astonishing mental trick.

SPELLING

Spelling the Aces

With a bit of memory work, you can perform a feat that simply *has* to be either magic or superb sleight of hand, but it's just subtlety. I developed a method of spelling the aces, using an adaptation of Gene Finell's "Free-Cut Principle."

You will need a full 52-card deck. Remove from the deck the four aces and the queen of spades, tossing them on the table face up. "The queen of spades is supposed to have magical properties," you say. "Let's see if she can accomplish anything with the four aces."

Holding the deck face down, rapidly fan through the cards in groups of three until you have nine cards. Even them up and place the group face down on the table to your left. Fan off ten cards the same way and place them to the right of the first pile. Do the same with another group of ten cards. Place the remaining cards to the right of all. "Whoops! I'll need another pile. Just a few cards will do." Take two cards from the top of your last pile and place these as a separate pile to the left of your first pile.

As you look at them, the piles are set up like this:

2   9   10   10   16

Place the ace of clubs face up on the second pile from the left. Place the ace of hearts face up on the pile to the right of it. Place the queen of spades face up on the pile to the right of that. Place the ace of spades face up on top of the farthest pile to the right. And place the ace of diamonds to the right of that pile (Illus. a). The aces go down in this order: clubs, hearts, spades, diamonds (CHaSeD), and the queen of spades goes in the middle of the aces.

Illus. a. The layout of the aces and the queen of spades

Say to a spectator, "Please turn the ace of clubs face down and place it on this pile." Indicate the two-card pile. "Now cut off some cards from this pile…" Indicate the pile from which the ace of clubs came. "…and place them on top of the ace of clubs."

Point to the ace of hearts. "Now turn this one face down and place it on top of this pile." Indicate the pile to your left of the pile on which the ace of hearts rests. "And cut off some cards from the pile…" Point to the pile from which the ace of hearts came. "…and place them on the ace of hearts."

In the same way, have him move the queen of spades to the next pile to your left. "But the queen of spades has work to do," you explain, "so let's keep her face up." Again cards are cut from the pile on which the queen of spades rested and are placed on top of the queen of spades.

The ace of spades is treated the same way, except that it's turned face down. Pick up the ace of diamonds, turn it face down, and place it on top of the pile on your far right, saying, "And I'll take care of the ace of diamonds myself."

Gather the cards from right to left, placing the pile on your far right on the pile next to it, placing both on the next pile, and so on.

"Three is a mystical number," you say, "so would you please cut the cards three times. This will give the queen of spades a chance to go through the deck and work her magic." After the cuts, pick up the cards and, holding them face down, fan through to the queen of spades. Set the pile which is *above* the queen onto the table. Take the queen in your right hand. "The question is, Did the queen do her work? We'll soon find out."

Toss the queen aside. Transfer the cards from your left hand to your right and drop them onto the pile on the table. Draw the deck toward you, picking it up. "Now let's see if you can spell out the aces. Here's what we'll do. We'll spell out an ace, dealing a card for each letter, and the ace should come out on the last letter. For instance, let's try the ace of hearts."

Spell *ace of hearts*, dealing one card into a face-down pile for each letter in the spelling. Turn the last card in the spelling face up. Let everyone see that it is the ace of hearts, then toss it aside face up with the queen of spades. Leave the dealt pile on the table.

Spectators will now choose the order in which the remaining aces are spelled. "What's another good ace?" you ask.

Whenever the ace of spades is named, you turn the deck face up and spell *ace of spades*, making a separate pile. Toss the ace of spades aside with the other ace(s) and queen of spades. Turn the dealt cards face down on the table. Turn over the cards in your hand so that they're back in the face-down dealing position.

You have only two aces to worry about—diamonds and clubs.

If diamonds is called before clubs:

Spell *ace of diamonds* from the top of the deck and toss it aside with the others. If the ace of spades has already been spelled, place all other piles, including the cards in your hand, on top of the pile just dealt. Turn the deck face up, and spell *ace of clubs.*

If the ace of spades has *not* already been spelled, set the deck down to the left of the pile just dealt. Place the pile you used to spell the ace of hearts on top of the pile just dealt. You now have two piles on the table. When the ace of spades is called, you pick up the pile on the left, turn it face up, and spell it.

If clubs is called before diamonds:

Spell *ace of clubs* from the top of the deck and toss it aside with the others. The ace of diamonds is now the third card from the top of the deck.

If the ace of spades has already been spelled, drop the deck on top of the pile you just made spelling the ace of clubs. Place the deck on top of one of the two other piles. Pick up the last pile and place it on top. You are now in position to spell *ace of diamonds* from the top.

If the ace of spades has not yet been spelled, set the remainder of the deck (the cards in your hand) to the left of the other piles. Say, "We'd better put the deck together." Point to the pile you just set down, saying to a spectator, "Please cut several cards from the top of this pile." This statement ensures that he will cut off at least three cards and that he won't cut past the ace of spades.

Pick up the pile you just made spelling the ace of clubs and place it on top of the remainder of the deck. On top of this, the spectator places the cards he just cut off. On top of all, place the other pile (the one you used to spell the ace of hearts). You are now in position to spell *ace of diamonds* from the face-down deck or *ace of diamonds* from the face-down deck or *ace of spades* from the face-up deck.

Apparently the aces are lost in the deck, yet you're able to spell them out *as called for*. It seems impossible. Yet mastery of this trick should take you no more than an hour or so of practice.

Evil Spell

For this stunt you need ten cards. From top to bottom, these are the cards: 3-5-A-7-9-2-queen spade-8-6-4. Except for the queen of spades, the suits are irrelevant. No reason not to make the setup in plain sight.

Spell the word "ace," transferring one card to the bottom for the "A" and another to the bottom for the "C." On "E" turn over the third card from the top, the ace, and toss it face up on the table. Spell out *two* and *three* the same way, tossing each into the pile begun with the ace.

Ask a volunteer to spell out *four*. When he turns over the last card, it is the queen of spades. "No, no," you say. "The queen of spades is bad luck. Here's the way you do it." Make sure the queen is returned to the top. Spell out *four*, tossing it on the table with the others. The spectator tries spelling *five* and gets the queen of spades, which is returned to the top. You spell *five* and toss the card on the table.

The spectator spells *six* and gets the queen of spades. "I keep telling you that's bad luck," you say, taking the cards back. You properly spell out the six. And then the seven.

The spectator fails with the eight, but you don't. The same with the nine. You are left with the queen of spades. Turn it over saying, "I know you really like the queen of spades. I'd give you permanent possession, but it would ruin the deck."

The spectator gets the queen of spades on the following deals: four, five, six, eight, and nine.

It's Magic

Set a thoroughly shuffled deck on the table. Ask Felix and Louise to help out. Say to Felix, "Please cut the deck into three fairly equal piles." When he's done, address Louise: "Choose one of those piles, and put the other two back into the card case."

About one-third of the deck is left on the table. Ask Louise to cut off a small pile from the packet. Felix takes the remaining cards.

Say to Louise, who has the smaller packet, "If I should perform a mysterious feat, would you say, 'It's magic'?" Whatever she replies, continue, "I'd like you to look at the bottom card of your packet, Louise. That's your chosen card." When she has done so, say, "Now spell out the words 'It's magic,' moving one card from the top to the bottom of your packet for each letter in the spelling."

Guide her through this.

Turn your attention to Felix. "You don't believe in magic, do you, Felix? You think all of this is trickery. In fact, you think that this is a dumb trick. What I'd like you to do is look at the bottom card of your packet and remember it." When he's done so, say, "Now please spell out the sentence 'This is a dumb trick.' Just as Louise did, move one card from the top to the bottom of your packet for each letter in the spelling."

Guide Felix, as well.

"Time for some elimination. I'd like each of you to deal your top card onto the table. Now place your next card underneath the packet. The next card goes on the table, and the next on the bottom of the packet. Keep going until you have only one card left, but please don't look at the card."

Help out as they perform their "down-under" deal. At last, each is holding one card face down.

"From the beginning, I haven't touched the cards, right? Nor did I have any way of knowing how many cards each of you would choose. So let's see if I'm magical...or not." Ask Louise to name her card. She then turns her last card over: it's the one she chose. Repeat the procedure with Felix.

Further Thoughts

• *The smaller pile must consist of no more than eight cards, and the large of no more than 16 cards. If you follow the above routine exactly, the numbers should work out.*

• *You can work up patter of your own, if you wish. Any*

eight-letter sentence will do for the smaller packet, and any 16-letter sentence will work for the larger packet.

*   *I n some respects the trick is even more effective when performed for one spectator. After you've eliminated two-thirds of the pack, the spectator cuts off a small pile from the remaining third. Offer the choice of the smaller packet or the larger packet. The pile which isn't chosen is placed in the card case with the other cards. Clearly, you proceed with the spectator looking at the bottom card and then spelling out "It's magic" with the smaller pile, or "This is a dumb trick" with the larger pile. This is followed by the down-and-under deal and the revelation of the chosen card.*

Note: The originator of this trick is (I believe) Patrick Duffie. Milt Kort introduced the trick to me.

Lots of Luck

Margie's a good sport, so ask her to shuffle the deck. Take it back, saying, "Poker is a game in which luck plays an important part, and we're going to need all kinds of luck for this experiment to work." Quickly push off five groups of five cards, tossing them on the table.

"Now we have five poker hands. Please pick up one of the hands, look it over, and take any card from it. Please show that card to everyone but me." Take the other four cards from her and place them on top of the deck. Continue: "Place the chosen card on top of one of the other piles, and place one of the remaining piles on top."

At this point, there are three piles on the table: two five-card piles and one 11-card pile in which the chosen card lies sixth from the top. You're holding the deck.

Spread the deck out face down directly in front of Margie. As you now speak, casually straighten the piles and place the two five-card piles on top of the 11-card pile. "I'd like you to draw out one card from the deck, but don't look at it just yet. Any card at all."

After Margie draws out the card, take the deck from her and set it on the table. Pick up the combined piles and drop them on top of the deck.

"Now we're going to spell out the name of the card you just picked out. We'll deal off one card for each letter in the spelling. We'll spell out the name of the card you just picked out. We'll deal off one card for each letter in the spelling. We'll spell out the name of the card exactly. For example, if you picked the queen of diamonds, we'd spell out (slowly) *queen of diamonds.* Don't worry; I'll show you how to do it."

Have her turn over the card. "Here's how you do it." Deal a card into a pile for each letter in the spelling of the card. Leaving the pile on the table, hand her the remainder of the deck. "Now you do it."

After she spells out the name of the card, take the deck from her and place it on top of the pile you spelled out. "We'll have to get rid of some more cards," you explain. "Pick up your pile, please. Now place the top card on the bottom. Then place the next card on the table." After she does so, say, "The next one on the bottom, and the next one on the table." She continues like this until only one card remains in her hand. Stop her, making sure she doesn't turn over the card.

"What's the name of your chosen card?" She gives the name; it's the card in her hand.

Note: Magician Wally Wilson showed me a spelling trick that he'd invented. I worked out a way to accomplish a similar effect using a different principle.

The Impossible Nine

There are not many card tricks in which the spectator handles the deck throughout. And, of these, very few are really effective. But this one is certainly one of the very best.

Ask Mary Lou to help out. "I don't know if you know this, but the number nine has peculiar qualities, not only in mathematics, but also in magic. So I would like you to shuffle the deck and then count off nine cards." She does so. "Shuffle those up and then look at the bottom card. This is your chosen card, so make sure you remember it. Now let's mix things up a bit. Place the top card on the bottom of your pile, and deal the next card on the table. Deal the next card under the pile, and the next one on the table." Have her continue to do this until all the cards are in a pile on the table. Ask Mary Lou to pick up the pile.

Turn your back, saying, "There is no way in the world that I can tell what or where your card is. Please think of the value of your card. For example, if you chose the five of spades, you would think of five. Now spell out the value of your card, dealing one card into a pile for each letter in the spelling. With *five*, you would deal one card on the table for 'F.' Deal another on top of it for 'I.' Deal another on top of that for 'V.' And deal another card on the pile for 'E.' Do this very quietly."

When she finishes say, "You have some cards left in your hand. Place these on top of the cards you dealt on the table. Pick up the entire pile. Now please spell out the word *of*, placing one card in a pile for each letter. In other words, deal two cards into a pile. Then place the rest of the cards on top of these, and pick up the entire pile."

When Mary Lou is done, continue, "In the same way, spell out your suit into a pile...either clubs, hearts, spades, or diamonds. If the suit were clubs, you would spell out C-L-U-B-S. Then place the rest of the cards on top of the pile and pick up the entire pile."

When Mary Lou is done, turn back to the group. "I think you'll agree that there's no way I could know the position of your card, nor the name of your card. After all, you could have spelled *two*, T-W-O, or *three*, T-H-R-E-E. Or any of the other values. And there's a big difference between the spelling of *clubs*, C-L-U-B-S, and *diamonds*, D-I-A-M-O-N-D-S. So how will we find your card? We'll have to resort to magic, or—as I like to refer to it—luck. I'll let you pick out something to spell. Mary Lou, do you believe in sorcery, mysticism?" If she says yes, say, "In other words, you believe in magic, right?" She does. So have her spell the word *magic*, dealing one card into a pile for each letter in the spelling. Ask her to name her card. Then have her turn over the last card she dealt.

But what if she answers no when you ask, "Mary Lou, do you believe in sorcery, mysticism?" You continue, "In other words, you think this is just a trick." Have her spell the word *trick*, as just described for the word *magic*. Since each word consists of five letters, the last card she deals will always be the chosen one.

How in the world does this thing work? The *under-down* deal brings the chosen card to third from the top. Using a nine-card pile, when you spell the complete name of any card, as described, the third card from the top will become the fifth card from the top.

You can reveal it any way you wish. The way I wish is to pretend to offer them a choice of words.

Further Thoughts

In the final phase of the trick, it's important that you ask, "Do you believe in sorcery, mysticism?" When she answers yes, it's perfectly natural that you should have her spell the word magic. If she answers no, you have her spell the word trick. And you have left her with the impression that she could have spelled out sorcery or mysticism. This is a small point, to be sure, but such touches are what turn a good trick into a miracle.

Note: As far as I know, Jim Steinmeyer discovered the principle used in this trick. This is basically the same as what he calls the Nine Card Problem, with a few of my own ideas thrown in.

SETUP

These tricks, in one way or another, require some preparation. In some instances, only a card or two must be placed in position. In others, a number of cards must be set up in advance. I believe that a really good trick is worth the bit of extra trouble.

Easy Opener

Remove the four aces from the deck. The ace of hearts goes on top of the deck, and the ace of diamonds goes on the bottom. The third card from the top is the ace of clubs, and the fourth card from the top is the ace of spades. Place the deck in its card case.

In performance, get a volunteer—Susie, for instance. Remove the deck from its case and set the case aside. Set the deck on the table. Make sure no one gets a peek at the bottom card.

"Susie, I'd like you to think of an ace—A-C-E, ace. It could be your favorite ace, or one you don't care for at all. Do you have an ace in mind? What is it?"

She names the ace. Suppose she names the ace of hearts. Say, "Put your hand on top of the deck and say, 'I want the top card to be the ace of hearts.'" She does so. Have her lift her hand. Turn over the top card, showing that her wish has come true.

Suppose she names the ace of clubs or the ace of spades. Say, "As I said, 'Ace, A-C-E.'" Pick up the deck. Spell out A-C-E, dealing one card from the top into a pile for each letter. If she named the ace of clubs, turn over the last card you dealt. If she named the ace of spades, turn over the current top card of the deck.

In all instances, gather up the cards and give them a good shuffle, destroying all the evidence. As you do so, patter about how incredible it is that she should have thought of that very ace. Go right into your next trick.

Note: Jay Ose often used this opening trick. I've made a few minor changes.

It's in Your Hands

The spectator handles the cards throughout an "impossible" location of a chosen card.

In preparation, remove all the clubs from the deck. From top to bottom, arrange them in this order:

10 9 8 7 6 5 4 3 2 A K Q J

The stack goes on the bottom of the deck, making the jack of clubs the bottom card.

In performance, set the deck face down on the table. Ask Bert to cut off a portion and shuffle it. Make sure he doesn't cut into your stack. "Replace the packet on top of the deck, please. Then take the top card, show it around, and replace it on the top."

When Bert's done, have him give the pack a complete cut. He, or someone else, gives the deck another complete cut.

Say, "Let's try something different. Turn the deck face up and give the cards a complete cut."

Have various spectators continue cutting the cards until a club shows up on the face of the deck. At this point, say, "That should be enough. The cards should be sufficiently mixed. Turn the deck face down, please."

You now know the position of the chosen card from the top. How? You add three to the value of the bottom card. Suppose a spectator has cut the six of clubs to the bottom. Add three to six, getting nine. The chosen card is ninth from the top. The ace is figured as one.

The obvious exception is when the jack, queen, or king of clubs is cut to the face of the deck. Just consider the jack as one, the queen as two, and the king as three—which should be easy to remember. So if the jack appears on the bottom, the chosen card will be on top; if the queen is on the bottom, the chosen card will be second from the top; and if it's the king, the chosen card will be third from the top.

As before, suppose the six of clubs was on the bottom. The deck is now face down on the table, and you know the chosen card is ninth from the top.

Harry Lorayne suggested this procedure: Have the spectator place his hand on the deck. Say, "Your card is 41st from the top, so please push down on the deck. Good! It's now 25th from the top. Push down a little harder. Hold it, hold it! You now have it 9th from the top. Any more pushing and you might push it out of the deck altogether. Let's check that 9th card and see if I'm right."

Have the spectator deal off nine cards into a pile. Ask him to name his card and then to turn over the last one dealt.

Further Thoughts

In the original version of this trick, the cards were stacked on the bottom in their natural order. This could give the trick away. A five shows up on the bottom, and the chosen card is five from the top. Not good.

Most Magicians

A simple setup is required: In a face-up pile place any six spades, other than those used in the spade royal flush. On top of these, place the ace of clubs, ace of hearts, and ace of diamonds, in any order. On top of these, in order, place the ace of spades, ten of spades, jack of spades, queen of spades, and king of spades. Place all on top of the deck.

Sidney will assist you. Explain, "Most magicians have a card selected like this. They either fan the cards out face down." Do so. "Or they fan the cards out face up." Do so, making sure you don't fan into your setup. "But I'm not most magicians." Close up the cards and turn them face down. Address Sidney: "I'd like you to give me a number between 10 and 20." He gives you the number. You deal that many cards into a face-down pile onto the table.

Tap the last card dealt. "Most magicians would have you take this card. But I'm not most magicians." Set the rest of the deck aside for the moment. Pick up the pile you just dealt. Let's suppose Sidney chose the number 15. "You had me deal out 15 cards. The digits are 1 and 5. Let's add them together. What do we get?" He replies. "Right, six." Deal six cards into a pile. Tap the last card you dealt and avert your head. "I'd like you to look at this card and show it around. Then replace it on top of the pile."

When he's done, place the pile in your hand on top of the pile on the table. Pick up the combined pile. "Let's mix these up a bit," you say. Remember the number the spectator chose? Now transfer that number of cards from the top to the bottom of the pile, moving one, two, or three cards each time. At the end of this "shuffle," the packet will be in precisely the same order. As you transfer cards, silently keep track. In our example, move 15 cards and then quit. "That should do it," you declare. Place the packet on top of the deck.

Spread out some of the top cards, saying, "Most magicians would fan through the deck and find your card. But..." At this point, you can either pantomime the rest of the statement or let the audience complete it for you. Say, "Instead, I'm going to see if the deck will tell me what your card is." Hold the deck to your ear and thoughtfully riffle the edges. Gradually you reveal that the card is black, a spade, the ace of spades. For each revelation, give the cards a little riffle.

Bring the deck forward and give a satisfied smile. Spectators will assume you're done.

Continue: "*Most* magicians would consider that enough. But..." Pause a moment, pointing your thumbs toward yourself. "Your card is the ace of spades. Let's spell *ace*." Spell *ace* into a pile, one card for each letter in the spelling. "Now, *spades*." To the right of the first pile, spell out *spades* in the same way. Turn over the top card of the deck. It's the ace of spades. Set the ace of spades face up beyond the two piles on the table.

Again, smile and give a little nod as though you're done. Pause, then say, "*Most* magicians..." You need not say any more. Point to the three-card pile on the table. "Here we have the ace pile." Turn the cards over, showing the three aces. "And here we have the spades pile." Turn over the other pile, showing the three aces. "And here we have the spades pile." Turn over the other pile, showing the six spades.

"Thank you, thank you," you say, taking a little bow. Pause.

"*Most* magicians..." Pause. "But we're not quite done," you say. "We have the ace of spades, and we'll require four more cards to make a poker hand." Deal off four cards from the top into a face-down pile. Now turn these cards over one by one, setting them in a row next to the ace of spades. As you do so, say "*Most* magicians would quit right now. And so will I...because you can't beat a royal flush in spades."

Note: This routine was originally developed by Stewart James. I like to do the J.W. Sarles version.

Sixes and Nines

Are you ready for a trick that has fooled some of the most knowledgeable card experts in the world? This is it. And Wally Wilson is the performer. He says that the basic trick is very old. But I was not familiar with it. Of course Wally has added a few wrinkles, along with his own special performance magic.

Preparation: Take the sixes and the nines from the deck. Places the sixes on top and the nines on the bottom.

Start by giving the deck a casual riffle shuffle. Let's assume you have the bottom half in your left hand and the top half in your right hand. Riffle off at least half a dozen cards with your left hand before you start meshing in the cards. This pretty much guarantees that half a dozen or so cards from your right hand will fall on top. It also guarantees that the sixes will still be on top and the nines on the bottom.

Lana will be delighted to assist you. Hand her the deck and say, "Lana, I'd like you to deal out the entire deck into four piles, going from left to right. Just deal them as though you were dealing out four hands in a card game—only neater."

When she finishes, continue: "Please pick up any one of the piles. Fan through the cards and take out any one you want. Put it aside for a minute while you set the pile back down. Now look at your card and show it around, but don't let me see its face."

After everyone but you has had a chance to see the card, go on: "Lana, put the card on top of any one of the piles." She does so. "Now if you want to, you can cut that pile. Or, if you prefer, place one of the other piles on top of it." If she cuts the pile on which her card sits, have her then stack all four piles in any order she wishes. If she does not cut that pile, have her proceed directly to the stacking of the piles.

The deck is now given at least two complete cuts. "You're the one who's been handling the deck, Lana, so it's certain that I have no idea where your card is." Spread the deck face up onto the table so that all the cards can be seen. "Nevertheless, some people suspect that I sneak cards out of the deck. I want you to notice that your card is still there. I'll look away while you check it out." As you say this, spread through the cards as though further separating them to provide a better view. Actually, you're looking for the sixes and nines. In one instance, you will find a six and a nine separated by one card. That is the one chosen by the spectator; remember it.

Mostly you'll find a six and a nine side by side. If Lana cut the packet before stacking the cards, you'll find a lone six and a lone nine somewhere. Just keep in mind that you're looking for the card that separates a six and a nine.

After you note this card, which will take just a few seconds, avert your head. "When you're done, Lana, gather up the cards, please, and then give them a good shuffle."

At this point, you can take the deck from Lana and reveal the card any way you wish. You could read her mind, for instance. Wally Wilson prefers this startling conclusion that includes an easy sleight I'd never seen before:

Fan through the cards, faces toward yourself. Cut some to the top. Fan through more cards and cut another small group to the top. Eventually, cut the cards so that the chosen card becomes the third card from the top. As you do all this, mutter things like, "It has to be here somewhere. I don't know. I *should* be able to figure this out." After the last cut, turn the deck face down. "I think I have it, Lana. But this is very diffi-

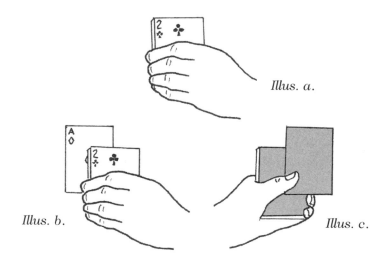

Illus. a.

Illus. b.

Illus. c.

cult, so I want four guesses. I probably won't need all four guesses, but you never know..."

The deck is in your left hand in the dealing position. Lift your left hand so that the bottom card faces the group (Illus. a). With your right thumb, pull up the top card diagonally. Move your right hand away so that about half the card is displayed (Illus. b). The left thumb holds the bottom left corner of the card (Illus. c). "Here's my first guess. Is this your card, Lana?" No, it isn't.

With the right hand, push the card back so that it is even with the others. At this point, you're still holding the cards in a vertical position. Lower the left hand to the regular dealing position. Deal the top card face down onto the table to your right.

Again raise the deck to a vertical position. Show the next card in the same way as before. Wrong again! Push the card

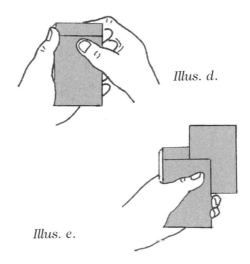

Illus. d.

Illus. e.

back, turn the deck to a horizontal position, and deal the top card onto the table to the left of the first card.

Once more raise the deck to a vertical position. This time, you'll perform a deceptive move that I call the *thumb glide*. Move the right hand up to the deck, as though to display the next card. As you chat with the spectators about your hopes for your third guess, move the top card down about half an inch with your right thumb. This is easily accomplished by using *very light* pressure (Illus. d). Then pull up the *second card from the top* and display it as you did the others (Illus. e). You're wrong again, of course. Push the card back with the right fingers and push the actual top card back into position with the right thumb. Now lower the deck and deal the top card onto the table to the left of the other two cards. You have cleverly and successfully managed to switch the card you showed for the chosen card.

You want to show a fourth card, but the spectators just saw the present top card. So you say, "Lana, this doesn't seem to be working. Maybe I'll have better luck if you cut the cards." Place the deck on the table and let her cut it. Pick the deck up and show a fourth card in the same way as you did the first two. Failure! Give Lana a look of mock disgust, saying, "Thanks a lot, Lana." The fourth card goes face down to the left of the others.

Place your right hand on the two cards on the right, and your left hand on the two cards to the left. Say, "Left or right, Lana?" Whatever she replies, lift your left hand. Pull the two cards beneath your right hand toward you. Turn one of them over. "So you say that this is not your card, Lana." Right. Turn the other card over. "And this isn't your card." Again, right.

"Hand me one of these cards, please." Indicate the two face-down cards on the table. If she hands you the card on your left, turn it over, saying, "And this isn't your card."

If she hands you the card on your right, take it, and set it in front of her. Turn over the other face-down card, saying, "And this isn't your card."

In either instance, the chosen card remains face down on the table. "So, what is your card, Lana?" She names it. Make a few magical gestures over the chosen card and then ask Lana to turn it over. At last you've located the chosen card.

What Do You Think?

A spectator merely *thinks* of a card and, in practically no time, you—with your incredible magical powers—locate it.

Preparation: First, unknown to all, put all the eights and nines on the bottom of the deck. The order of these placed cards doesn't matter.

Ready? Say to Greta, "I'd like you to think of a number *between* one and ten." (Be sure to say "between," because you don't want her to choose one or ten.) "Now I'll show you ten cards one at a time. Please remember the card that lies at the number you thought of."

Avert your head as you hold up the top card, face toward Greta. At the same time, say, "One." Take the next card in front of the first and show it to Greta, saying, "Two." Continue through the tenth card. Replace the ten cards onto of the deck. They are, of course, in the same order.

"Great, I'm going to put these cards behind my back and perform an astonishing feat. I'm going to put your chosen card in a position where you yourself will locate it with a randomly chosen card."

Put the deck behind your back. Take off the top card and put it on the bottom. Turn the deck face up. To yourself, *very quietly* count off the nine bottom cards, one on top of the other. Place this packet on top of the deck. Turn the deck face down and bring it forward. You now have an indifferent card on top, followed by the eights and nines.

"Okay, great, everything is ready. All I need to know is the number you thought of." She names the number. Let's say the number is 6. Count aloud as you deal five cards onto the table. When you say "six" aloud, lift off the sixth card, turn it over, and continue to hold it. It will be either an 8 or a 9. Whichever it is, announce its value, and say, "Let's hope that this card will help us find your card."

If the card is an 8, place it face up onto the pile you dealt off. In another pile, deal eight cards, counting aloud. Ask Greta to name her card. Turn over the last card dealt. It is the one she thought of.

If the last card you lift off is a 9, call attention to it, and then turn it face down on top of the deck. Deal off nine cards, counting aloud. As before, the last card will be the one chosen.

Summary

When the spectator gives the number she thought of, you deal off one less than this number, counting aloud. When you name the last number of the count, you hang on to the card. Turn it over, still holding it. If it's an 8, drop it on top of the pile you just dealt; deal off eight cards from the rest of the deck and turn over the last card. If it's a 9, replace it face down on top of the deck; deal off nine cards from the deck and turn over the last card.

The Ideal Card Trick

Here's the ideal card trick: A card is selected, you do something miraculous with it, and no skill is required. Here we have the invention of U. F. Grant, a creative giant in the field of magic.

Preparation: Place any 4 face up fourth from the bottom of the deck.

Daphne sure is a good sport, so fan the cards out and ask her to select a card. Make sure, of course, that you do not spread the cards out near the bottom; no need to disclose the face-up 4. Have her show the card around and then replace it on top of the deck. Give the deck a complete cut and set it on the table.

"Daphne, I am going to attempt a feat that is nearly impossible. I am going to try to turn a card face up in the middle of the deck. Will it be your card? Oh, no, that would be too easy. Instead, I will try to turn over a card that will tell us where your card is. I can't believe how tough this is going to be."

Pick up the deck and give it a little riffle at the ends. "I hope that works." Fan through the cards until you come to the face-up 4. "Ah, here we have a face-up card, a 4." Set the cards above the 4 onto the table. Lift off the 4 and place it, still face up, on the table. "So let's count off four cards." Deal off four cards, counting aloud. Place your finger on the last card dealt off. "What was the name of your card, Daphne?" She names it, and you turn it over.

ACES

It's Out of My Hands

How about yet another trick in which the spectator does all the work? Sprinkled among others, such tricks seem to be especially magical.

Edgar is an excellent card player, so you might ask him to take the deck and shuffle it. Continue: "Please go through the cards and take out the four aces."

When Edgar turns the deck face up, take note of the bottom card and remember it; this is your key card. Then you banter with the group, paying no particular attention as he tosses the aces out. (If he somehow manages to change the bottom card, however, take note of the new bottom card. This is your key card.)

The aces are face up on the table. Ask Edgar to turn the deck face down. "Now, Edgar, put the aces in a face-down row, and then deal three cards on top of each ace." When he finishes, say, "Gather the piles up, one on top of the other, and put them on top of the deck."

Then: "Please give the deck a complete cut." Make sure that as he begins the cut he lifts off at least 16 cards. Usually, the completed cut will leave the aces somewhere around the middle of the deck.

"In a moment, we're going to make some piles, Edgar. Which pile would your prefer—pile 1, pile 2, pile 3, or pile 4?" Whatever he replies, repeat his choice so that everyone will remember.

"Please deal the cards slowly into a face-up pile. If all goes well, I'll get a strong feeling as to when you should stop."

At a certain point (described below) you tell him to stop. Then: "Deal the next four cards into a face-down row. Then deal the next four cards into a row, right on top of the first four cards. Do the same with the next four cards, and then four more." Make sure he deals the cards across in a row each time. As he deals each group of four, count, "One, two, three, four."

Call the group's attention once more to the number of the pile that Edgar chose. "Don't forget. At no time have I touched the cards. Would you please turn over the pile you picked." He does so, and there are the four aces.

How you do it: When Edgar deals the cards out face up, you know exactly where to stop him. You watch for your key card, the original bottom card of the deck. To make sure the aces get into the proper pile, you simply subtract the number of the chosen pile from 4. For instance, if Edgar chooses pile 4, you subtract 4 from 4, getting zero. After he turns over the key card, you allow no more cards to be dealt out face up. He immediately begins forming the four piles.

If he chooses pile 3, you subtract 3 from 4, getting 1. So you let one more card be dealt face up after the key card.

If he chooses 2, you subtract 2 from 4, getting 2. Therefore, two more cards are dealt after the key card.

If he chooses 1, you subtract 1 from 4, getting 3. So three more cards are dealt after the key card.

Double or Nothing

Start by tossing the four aces face up onto the table. "Here we have the four aces, as you can see. Now I'm about to play a game of *Double or Nothing*. I'll give out real money to the winner. Whoever volunteers will risk nothing whatever. Do I have a volunteer?"

You choose Hannibal from the multitude of eager volunteers.

"Congratulations, Hannibal. Just by volunteering, you have already won. To win even more, you'll have to keep track of the aces."

Arrange the aces in a face-down row. Fan off three cards from the top of the deck and place them on top of one of the aces. Tap the pile of four cards. "For double or nothing, keep track of this ace, Hannibal."

Place the pile of four cards on top of the deck. As you do so, get a break with your left little finger beneath the top card of the four. Double-cut this card to the bottom of the deck. (See *Double-Cut*, page 15.)

"Where's that first ace, Hannibal? Is it on the bottom?" Turn the deck over, showing the bottom card. "No. Is it on top?" Turn over the top card, showing it, and then turn it face down again. "No. So where is it?" You coach Hannibal by saying, "Somewhere in the mmmm...somewhere in the mid..." Whatever he responds, you say, "Right! Somewhere in the middle of the deck. You've doubled your money! You now have two...pennies." This should get a chuckle. "Double or nothing, Hannibal. Let's try four pennies." Fan off the top three cards and place them on another ace. Pick up the four cards and place them on top of the deck. Double-cut the top card to the bottom of the deck.

"Where's that ace, Hannibal? Is it on the bottom?" Show the bottom card, as before. "No. Is it on top?" Show the top card and replace it. "No. So where is it?" Hannibal should have no trouble this time. "That's right," you say, "somewhere in the middle of the deck. You now have eight pennies. Let's try for 16."

The procedure this time is a little different. Fan off three cards from the top of the deck and place them on top of one of the two remaining aces. Pick up the four-card pile. Carefully even it up; you're going to turn the pile face up and you don't want anyone to get a glimpse of the other aces in the pile. *Now* turn the pile over, showing the ace on the bottom. Place the pile face down on top of the deck. "You *must* know where that ace is. Obviously, it isn't on the bottom." Show the bottom card of the deck, as before. "And it isn't on top." Show the top card and return it to the top.

At this point, double-cut the top card to the bottom. "So, for 16 pennies, where is it?" As usual, it's somewhere in the middle of the deck. "For 32 pennies, Hannibal—where are all four aces?"

Chances are he'll say, "In the middle of the deck." If he does, say, "Not exactly. They're right here." Deal off the top four cards face up. They are the aces. (Whatever he responds, proceed the same way.)

Pause a moment for audience appreciation. "But that was close enough, Hannibal. You still win the 32 pennies." Take out your wallet. "Do you have change for a big bill?"

Note: I believe that the basic principle used here was developed by Stewart James, and Ray Boston adapted it to a four-ace trick. My version creates great spectator interest and has an extremely strong climax.

A Good Cut of Chuck

Fan through the deck, saying, "I'll need the four aces." When you come to a 5, cut the cards so that it becomes second from the top of the deck. "They have to be here somewhere." Toss the aces face up onto the table as you come to them.

Arrange the aces in a face-up row. Turn the deck face down. Cut from the top about a quarter of the cards and place the face-down packet below the ace on the left. (The packet is placed nearer to you.) Cut from the top about a third of the remaining cards and place the packet below the second ace from the right. Cut off about half the remaining cards and place this packet below the second ace from the left. Place the remaining cards below the ace on the right. In other words, about a quarter of the deck is below each ace, with the original top portion of the deck being the pile on the left.

Pick up the packet on the left. (As you recall, the second card from the top of this packet is a 5.) Turn the packet face up and fan through the cards so that you can see which card is sixth from the original top. Pick up the ace on the left and place it to the right of this card. So the first ace is now seventh from the original top of the packet you're holding in your left hand (Illus. a). Close up the packet.

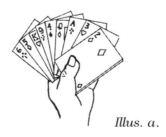

Illus. a.

With your right hand, pick up the packet which is now on the left. Turn it face up and place it on top of the cards in your left hand. Pick up the ace on the left and place it on top of the cards in your left hand.

Fan back through the cards, showing how widely the two aces are separated. When you fan back to the face of the packet, get a break with the tip of your left little finger under the fourth card from the face. Give the cards a double-cut, cutting the three cards above the break to the back of the face-up group. (See *Double-Cut*, page 15.)

Pick up the present packet on the left, turn it face up, and put it on top of the face-up cards in your left hand. Reach with your right hand to pick up the ace now on the left. As you do so, secure a break under the top card with your left little finger. The action of reaching for the ace provides plenty of misdirection. Pick up the ace and place it face up on top of the packet. You're now holding a little-finger break beneath the top two cards of the packet. In a double-cut, move these two cards to the back of the face-up packet.

Handle the last packet and ace in exactly the same way as you did the third packet and ace.

The cards from the top are now in this order, x standing for any card:

x A x A x x x A x 5 x x x x A

Even up the cards and hold them up so that all can see that no cards are sticking out and that you're holding no breaks. *But don't say anything to that effect!*

Turn the deck face down.

"Let's see if I can find any of the aces."

Lift the deck with your right hand. Turn your hand over, showing that the bottom card of the deck is not an ace. Place the deck face down into your left hand. Push off the top card with your left thumb. Take this card with your palm-down right hand, thumb at the inner end, fingers at the outer end. Lift it and show its face (Illus. b). As you retain the card to the top of

Illus. b.

the deck, you easily hold a break with your right thumb between the card and the rest of the deck, while the right thumb holds the break along with the inner end of the deck. You're now going to perform a triple-cut, which is a variation of *The Double-Cut*, on page 15. The left hand takes about a *third* of the cards from the bottom and places them on top, still retaining the break held by your right thumb. Again with the left hand, move a third of the cards from the bottom to the top. Now the left hand takes the remainder of the cards below the break and puts them on top. The upshot is that the top card which showed is now on the bottom, and an ace is on top of the deck.

Turn the ace over, showing it, and place it face up onto the table.

To get a second ace, repeat all these moves. Finally, show the ace on top and place it onto the table next to the first ace.

Turn the deck face up and fan out several cards at the bottom, showing that there's no ace there. Turn the deck face down. Fan out three cards from the top (Illus. c). Take them in your right hand. Hold your hand up, displaying the faces. As you replace them face down on top, get a break beneath them with the tip of your left little finger.

Illus. c.

Once more you perform the triple-cut, bringing these three cards to the bottom. On top is an ace, which you turn over and deal onto the table next to the other two.

Lastly, you repeat the moves you used for the first two aces. This time, when you turn over the top card, it turns out to be a 5. "A five!" you declare, clearly disappointed. "We might as well use it."

Set the 5 aside face up. Slowly deal five cards from the top into a pile on the table, counting aloud. Turn over the last card dealt. It's the final ace.

"Thank goodness," you declare, placing the final ace next to the other three.

Note: I don't know who originated this trick, but it was shown to me by Chuck Golay, who I'm sure added touches of his own. It's that rare trick that requires little skill but gives the impression of incredible dexterity.

Four for Aces

You ask four spectators to help out. Explain to them, "We're about to conduct a scientific experiment. We'll try to find out if you four have *anything* in common. First, I'll give each of you an ace and five other cards."

Do so. "I'd like you all to shuffle your six cards. Mix them up really well."

When they finish, continue: "Please, each of you fan your cards out so that only you can see their faces. Notice what number your face is from the top. Please remember that number. Now turn your cards face down. Move three cards from the top to the bottom of your pile." Pause. "Remember that number that I asked you to remember? Please move that number from the top to the bottom of your pile." Pause. "Just for good measure, move one more card from the top to the bottom."

Address just one spectator: "Please gather up the piles in any order you wish." As he gathers the piles one on top of the other in any order, make sure he does not misconstrue your instructions to include shuffling. Take the cards from the spectator.

"Continuing the experiment, we'll need six piles." Deal the cards into six piles as though dealing six hands of cards. The second pile is critical, for it consists of all four aces. You are about to force the selection of this pile through a so-called magician's choice.

"We'll need to make some choices here." Ask Buster, one of your assistants, to help out.

Spread your right hand out and place it on the table so that it touches the three piles on the right. Put your left hand on the table so that it touches the three piles on the left.

Address Buster, "What'll it be, right or left?"

Whatever he replies, gather up the three piles on *your* right and set them aside.

Turn to Maxine. Gesture toward the three remaining piles. "Please hand me a pile, Maxine."

If she hands you the pile containing the aces, fine. Say, "I think it's quite obvious that you four have a psychic bond." Deal the aces face up one at a time.

Otherwise, set the pile aside with the other three you discarded.

It's Pam's turn. "Pam, I'd like you to pick a pile."

She will either pick up one of the two remaining piles, or she will point to one. If she chooses the one containing the aces, discard the other, saying, "Excellent choice, Pam." Proceed to the end as described above.

If she chooses the other, discard it. Point to the remaining pile, saying, "And that leaves us with this pile." Pick it up and proceed to the end.

Summary

1. *Four spectators are each given six cards, including an ace.*

2. *They are given these instructions:*

A. *Mix your cards.*

B. *Fan them out so that only you can see the faces and note what number your ace is from the top. Remember that number.*

C. *Turn your cards face down. Move three cards rom the top to the bottom of your pile.*

D. *Recall the number you were to remember? Move hat number from the top to the bottom of your pile.*

E. *For good measure, move one more card from the top to the bottom of your pile.*

3. *One spectator gathers up the piles in any order.*

4. *You deal the cards into six piles. Through "magician's choice," you force the selection of pile 2, which contains all four aces.*

Further Thoughts

• *If you wished, you could have the spectators do all the moves. But with this trick, I like to handle the cards, thus offering the possibility that the trick is not totally automatic.*

• *Why does this trick work? If we change the order of the instructions, I think the answer will be apparent.*

The spectator has noted the number of his ace from the top of his packet. Suppose your instructions follow this order:

1. *Remember that number I asked you to remember. Please move that number from the top to the bottom of your pile. (Where is the ace? On the bottom of the pile.)*

2. *Move three cards from the top to the bottom of your pile. (Where is the ace? Third card from the top.)*

3. *Just for good measure, move one more card from the top to the bottom. (The ace is now second from the top.)*

Note: Les Nixon is responsible for the first mention I've found of this startling puzzler.

CLOCKS

Tick Tock Trick

You deal twelve cards in a face-up circle, each card indicating an hour on the clock. Start with one o'clock and deal around to twelve o'clock, calling off each number (or time) as you deal. The card at twelve o'clock should be pushed a little above the circle so that the spectators will have no trouble telling what card lies at what time. The queen of spades is placed in the middle and is dubbed "the card of mystery." A spectator mentally selects one of the cards and remembers the time at which it lies.

Turn your back and tell the spectator to quietly count from the deck a number of cards equal to the hour at which his selected card lies. If his card lies at five o'clock, he counts off five cards. These cards are placed in the spectator's pocket or are otherwise concealed.

Now gather up the cards, apparently casually. Chat with the spectators as you do so. Pick up "the card of mystery" first and place it face up in your left hand. Pick up the rest of the cards in reverse order, starting with the card at twelve o'clock. The last one placed face up in your left hand is the card at one o'clock. Put these cards face down on top of the deck.

Note: To my delight, this trick of mine appeared in the September 1949 issue of Conjurors' Magazine. This trick is always received well and it is a nice change of pace from more conventional effects.

The Clock Strikes Again

The trick, my invention, is colorful, quick, and extremely puzzling. Spectators seem to enjoy tricks in which you lay out cards in a clock formation.

Annie needs to know everything, so explain to her, "I'll need eleven spot cards to make up a clock. You'll furnish the twelfth card."

Without letting the spectators see the cards, find a 2 of any suit and place it face down on the table. Place on top of it a face-down 4. Follow this with a 6, an 8, and a 10. Next comes an ace, followed by a 3, a 5, a 7, a 9, and another 5.

So from the bottom up, you have 2, 4, 6, 8, 10, A, 3, 5, 7, 9, 5. This should be easy enough to remember. First come the even spot cards from low to high, followed by the odd spot cards from low to high, and then an extra 5. The suits don't matter.

Hand Annie the rest of the deck. "Please pick out any face card." You take it from her, announce its name, and place it face down on top of the packet. Give the packet a cut. Have Annie cut the cards. Other spectators may cut as well. When they are satisfied, take the cards back.

At this point, you may decide to try out some patter provided by Wally Wilson: "*Tempus fugit,* Latin for 'time flies,' is found on many timepieces. You may have heard the expression that 'time flies like an arrow,' or that 'fruit flies like rotten bananas.' Let's see if the seconds will fly by as we try to end up with the face card you selected."

Deal the cards *clockwise* into a face-down circle. "This is a clock. But we're not going to know which way the clock is facing until someone chooses a twelve-o'clock card." Have Annie pick a twelve-o'clock card. You move it slightly out of line. "Now please pick a time. We're going to hope for very good luck now."

Annie picks a time. You start with one o'clock and, touching each card in order, count to the selected time. Turn this card face up. If it turns out to be the face card, quit; you've just performed a spectacular trick. Chances are rather strong, however, that she'll pick a spot card.

You say, "You have chosen the twelve-o'clock card without any help from me, and you've selected a time. The cards were cut several times. Despite all this, I have a strong feeling that you'll find it extremely difficult to find the face card you selected. In fact, you might just find it last."

Explain that, starting with the next card in order, she is to count clockwise, moving the number of cards indicated by the value shown on her selection. For example, suppose Annie picks three o'clock. Let's suppose that it's a 6. She starts with the next card, the one which stands for four o'clock, and counts that as 1. She counts to 6, touching a succeeding card for each count, landing on the card at nine o'clock. She turns this card over. (It will be a 5.) Starting with the next card and moving clockwise, she counts five cards, turning over the fifth card. She continues in this manner until only one card remains face down.

"Only one card remains—the face card that you chose." Turn the face card over and place it face up in the middle of the circle.

After everyone has had a chance to see the display, gather up the cards. You don't want the group to have a chance to study the pattern. Don't hurry, but don't dally either.

Further Thoughts

• *You may want to speed the trick up by counting and turning over the cards yourself.*

• *I've never had a spectator figure out the trick. Still, if you're afraid that a brilliant friend might discern the pattern, you might try this: After the spectator turns over his first card, announce the value and give your speech about what you hope will happen. Then fan through the face-up deck to a face card. Cut the cards so that this becomes the bottom card of the deck. This sends all the spot cards below the face card to the top of the deck, thus making it easier to find succeeding face cards. Take the face card and place it face up on top of the spectator's face-up card. "I'm going to cover your choice with a face card for luck. If I'm right, when you turn over your last card, we'll have all face cards."*

When the spectator counts to his next card, you fan through to the next face card and cut the cards so that it becomes the bottom card of the deck. (You do this for each succeeding face card.) This face card goes face up on the card he counted to. You continue on. Eventually all the cards are covered with face cards and one card is face down: the face card he chose at the beginning.

Hickory-Dickory-Dock

Fan through the deck and remove the queen of spaces. Toss it onto the table face up. "Let's try an experiment in which we'll use some cards to form a clock. But first: As you know, all women have mysterious powers, and queens have more than most. In the deck of cards, the queen of spades has more power than any other card. Naturally, she'll serve as twelve o'clock, the highest number. And just maybe, she'll help bring about a magical result."

You'll need someone who's fairly adept with cards to assist you, so ask Fred to help out.

Casually count off 11 cards and hand them to him. "Fred, I'd like you to mix those cards thoroughly. When you're satisfied, look at the bottom card and remember it. You may show it to others so they can share the fun."

After he finishes, continue: "Now we want that card mixed in among the others, so you get a choice. Do you want to do the down-under shuffle, or the under-down shuffle?"

If you say this fast enough, Fred is bound to be confused. So explain slowly: "If you choose the down-under shuffle, you place the first card down and put the next card under the packet. The next card goes down, and the next one under the packet, until all the cards are on the table.

"If you choose the under-down shuffle, the first card goes under the packet and the next one onto the table, the next one under the packet, and the next one onto the table, until all the cards are on the table.

"Either way, you'll give the cards two shuffles of the same sort. So which do you prefer, down-under or under-down?"

Make sure he understands. Have him perform one of the two

types of shuffle. He then picks up the cards and does the same kind of shuffle again. His chosen card is now either on the top or bottom of the pile of 11 cards. It's easy to remember which. If he performed two *under*-down deals, his card is *under*, that is, it's on the bottom. Otherwise, it's on top.

You take the cards from Fred and deal them face down into a clock formation, starting from the face-up queen of spades, which is at twelve o'clock. If his card is on the bottom (that is, he performed the *under*-down shuffles), you start at one o'clock and deal around to eleven o'clock. If his card is on top, you start at eleven o'clock and deal backward to one o'clock. Clearly, in either instance, the chosen card is at eleven o'clock. You do *not* say the numbers aloud as you place the cards down.

"Pick any time you wish," you say to Fred. In the unlikely event that he says 11, "Are you sure you want that? You can choose any time at all." He'll probably stick with his choice. Touch the card at one o'clock, saying, "One." Continue around the circle, stating each number as you touch the appropriate card. After landing on 11, say, "What was the name of your chosen card?" He names it. Turn over the card at 11 o'clock. Sure enough, it's the chosen one. Just another of your many miracles.

But Fred is much more likely to name some other number. "We'll count that number out again and again, eliminating one card each time by turning it face up. If we're in luck, your chosen card will be the last one eliminated." Point to the face-up queen of spades. "As you can see, the queen of spades is already eliminated, so we'll not use her at all in the counting. Besides, she'd be insulted. Everyone knows you can't count on a queen." Pause, providing everyone the chance to give you an appropriately dirty look. "If you want to, Fred, you can change your mind and choose another time."

It really doesn't matter. The eleventh card will be the last one eliminated, regardless.

Let's say that Fred chooses five o'clock. Move the queen of spades well outside the circle so that you don't mistakenly count it (Illus. a). Then count aloud from one o'clock to five o'clock, touching the appropriate cards as you go. Turn the card at five o'clock face up.

Start with the next card, the one at six o'clock, and count to five aloud once more, moving clockwise and touching one card for each number. You land on ten o'clock. Turn that card face up.

Illus. a.

Start with the card at eleven o'clock and count off five again, making sure you don't count the queen of spades. You land at the card at four o'clock. Turn it face up.

Continue, remembering this: *Count every card, whether it is face up or face down.* The obvious exception is the queen of spades, which is never counted.

Eventually, only one card is face down. Ask Fred to name his selection. He does. Sure enough, his chosen card is the last one to be eliminated.

Further Thoughts

In this trick, you always end up with the eleventh card. If you make a circle of 13 cards, you'll end up with the thirteenth card. In fact, if you make a circle of any prime number of cards and follow the procedure, you'll end up with the card at the prime number. A prime number is any number that can't be divided evenly by any numbers other than itself or the number 1. Examples: 1, 2, 3, 5, 7, 11, 13, 17, 19, 23, 29, etc.

Note: I consulted my friends Wally Wilson and Milt Kort about the possibility of improving the previous trick *(The Clock Strikes Again)*. They came up with a clever adaptation of an old principle in which you always end up with the bottom card of 11 cards. Wally figured that the principle could easily be adapted to a clock trick, and Milt verified this. Using their idea, I worked out a way to locate a selected card. Thus, two great minds and my mind combined to offer this colorful, effective trick.

My Time Is Your Time

Start by handing Jack the deck and asking him to give it a shuffle. When he's done, say, "It's no secret, Jack, that the number 12 is quite significant. For instance, there are the 12 signs of the zodiac, the 12 months in a year, the 12 hours shown on the clock, and so on. So please count off 12 cards into a pile."

After he does so, take the rest of the deck from him. "Please pick up your 12 cards, Jack."

You have placed the remainder of the deck into your left hand, preparatory to making an overhand shuffle. As Jack picks up his cards, you let the deck tilt slightly back toward the palm of your left hand (Illus. a). Casually look down at your hands, sneaking a peek at the bottom of the deck.

Illus. a.

This is important: Begin to give the cards an overhand shuffle *before* you say, "Shuffle your cards like this."

Jack shuffles his packet. You complete your overhand shuffle by shuffling off the last several cards individually, thus bringing the card you peeked at to the top of the deck. (You must know the name of the top card of those you're holding. Clearly, any other sneaky way you want to do it is just fine.)

Set your cards onto the table. Avert your head and tell Jack, "Please cut off some of your cards and put them into your pocket. But don't pay attention to the number as you do this."

When he's done, say, "Put the rest of your cards on top of the deck and even up the deck."

You once more face the group.

"Neither of us knows how many cards you have in your pocket, right? Now I'd like you to pick up the deck and count out 12 cards, dealing them into a pile."

He does this.

"Set the rest of the deck aside. Pick up the pile of 12 cards and deal it out, forming a clock. The first card will be at one o'clock, and the last will be at 12 o'clock."

The clock has been formed. Move the card marking 12 o'clock an inch or two out of line as you comment, "So this is 12 o'clock."

Turn away. "I'd like you to take those cards from your pocket, Jack, and count them. But don't tell me the number."

He counts the cards.

"You have your number? Look at the card that lies at that time. For example, if you had four cards in your pocket, you'd look at the card that lies at four o'clock. Show the card around and then replace it face down. When you're done, put the cards that you had in your pocket back on top of the deck."

You turn back and reveal the chosen card any way you wish.

Remember that card you peeked at? Well, that's the one he chose. You can have him gather up all the cards and shuffle them. Then you can go through the deck and locate the card, or else read the spectator's mind.

My favorite conclusion is this: Before I turn back, I have the spectator gather up all the cards and shuffle them. When I face the group, I take the deck, riffle the ends a few times, and then rub it against my wristwatch.

"Since you used a clock in choosing a card, maybe my timepiece will help me identify it." I set the deck onto the table.

I hold my wristwatch to my ear and listen to it as it slowly gives me the color, the suit, and the value of the selected card.

Note: Wally Wilson showed me yet another clock trick. This one is extraordinarily deceptive.

FUN

The Cutting Edge

When you have a chance to do so unobserved, turn the bottom card of the deck face up and then turn the entire deck over. You have one card face down on top while all the others are face up.

Approach a spectator, saying, "Please cut off a pile of cards, and I will *instantly* name the card you cut to."

The pile is cut off; you see the face-up card and name it. After taking the cards back from the spectator, restore the deck to its proper order. Some will think you have actually performed a trick; most will think you're just silly.

Twin Picks

Cheryl cuts off a small pile from the top of the deck. Anthony cuts off a larger pile. Both count their cards and remember the number. The two piles are put together and shuffled.

You take the cards. Go to Cheryl, saying, "I want you to note and remember the card at your number. Take off the top card at your number. Take off the top card and show it to her, saying, "One." Place the card face down on the table. Show her the rest of the cards, stating each number, and placing the cards on top of one another on the table. After you show the last card, slide it under the rest, scooping up the others. It now becomes the bottom card of the group.

Go to Anthony, asking him to note the card at his number. Show him the cards in the same way you did for Cheryl. Gather up the cards. Say, "At the count of three, I'd like you both to state the name of your card loudly and clearly. Despite the confusion, I will be able to distinguish the names of both chosen cards. One, two, three!"

They both name the same card.

"Good! I won't have to bother."

A Little Error

This is the only one of the group that is a genuine trick. The basic principle has been used in quite a few tricks. My application is both deceptive and amusing.

You'll need the assistance of two spectators. Beth and Randy seem particularly eager, so you choose them. No matter how bright Beth and Randy are, they might have trouble with your directions, so it's best to start things off with a demonstration.

"Here's what I'm going to ask you to do. Beth, I'm going to ask you to shuffle the deck and then deal as many cards as you wish into two equal piles."

As you explain, shuffle the deck, and deal out two equal piles of at least ten cards each.

"You keep one pile, Beth, and push the other one over to Randy."

"Each of you will cut off some cards from your pile." Indicate that they should do so.

"Then you'll look at the bottom card of those you've cut off. That'll be your chosen card." It's best at this point that they do *not* look at their bottom card; you don't want them to confuse that card with the one they'll choose in a moment.

"Beth, you'll place that pile you cut off on top of the pile that Randy has on the table." Take the pile from her and place it on top of Randy's pile on the table. "And Randy, you'll place the cards you cut off on top of Beth's pile on the table." Take the cards he's holding and place them on top of Beth's pile on the table.

"Put the piles together by putting either pile on top." Demonstrate. "And then each of you gives the combined pile a complete cut." Have them do so.

Hand the cards to Beth. "Don't worry if you don't remember it all. I'll talk you through it. Start by shuffling the deck and then dealing out two equal piles onto the table." When she deals the cards down, you keep silent count of the number that goes into one of the piles. Let's assume that she deals two piles of nine cards each. *Remember this number.*

Turn your back and continue your directions. "Beth, place one of the piles in front of you, and push one of them in front of Randy. Now I'd like each of you to shuffle your pile and put it back onto the table." Pause. "Each of you please cut off some cards from your pile and look at the bottom card of those you cut off. Remember that card, because later I'm going to read your mind and tell you exactly what that card is. Are you still holding your cut-off pile, Beth?" Yes, she is. "Did you look at the bottom card?" She did. "All right. Place that pile on top of the cards that Randy left on the table." Pause briefly.

"Randy, are you still holding your cut-off pile?" Yes, he is. "Will you remember the bottom card of that pile?" Yes, he will. "Can you guess where I want you to place that pile? That's right. Please put it on top of the cards that Beth left on the table."

After another brief pause, continue: "Beth, please put one pile on top of the other; it doesn't matter which goes on top."

Turn back to the group. "Randy, please give the pile a complete cut." When he finishes, say, "Beth, I'd like you to cut the cards also."

After she's done, pick up the packet, saying, "Eventually, I'm going to reveal the names of both your cards. But I'll start with Beth. Please concentrate on your card, Beth, as I look at the faces of these cards."

Fan through the cards, faces toward you. After a moment, say, "Are you concentrating, Beth? I'm not getting it. Just think of the suit of your card." Fan through again. "No, it's not working. Instead, Beth, just think of the...of the..." Your eyes light up. With a snap of your fingers, you say, "I've got it! I've got it! Just think of the *value* of your card."

Go through the cards again, rather halfheartedly this time. "No, I just can't get it, Beth. What's the name of your card?"

She names the card; let's suppose it's the four of diamonds. You remember that in the beginning nine cards were in each pile. Again, you fan through the cards, faces toward you. When you get to the four of diamonds, start counting with the *next* card. Count to nine, the number of cards that were in each pile. (If you run out of cards before you complete the count, simply continue counting with the card at the face of the packet.) The card that you land on is the other chosen card. Let's say this is the six of spades. Without letting anyone see its face, remove it from the packet and place it face down onto the table. As you do this, you demonstrate that you're full of confidence again. "All right, one down and one to go." (It's important that you say this. Without making a big deal of it, you strongly imply that you've just placed the four of diamonds onto the table.)

"Randy, please concentrate on your card." Extend the probing process with Randy for a brief time; unfortunately, you're still unsuccessful. Then you say, "I've got it! I knew I'd get it." Brief pause. "Yes, a *headache* is what I've got." Pause for the laugh or, of course, the wide-eyed stares. "Okay, Randy, what's your card?"

"Six of spades," he says.

"No wonder I couldn't get your card. I really goofed up. I put the wrong card onto the table."

Turn the card on the table over. The six of spades.

It may take the group several seconds to figure out that you've done something quite magical.

RED AND BLACK

The One & Only

Let's assume you're using a deck with blue backs. You're going to use 16 cards, 8 of the black suits and 8 of the red suits. The values and the specific suits don't matter. One of the red-suit cards, however, will be from a different deck and will have a *red back*. Let's say this card is the queen of hearts.

Remove the packet of 16 cards from your pocket and turn it face up. Deal the cards out face up. This is how they'll appear from the spectator's view:

B	R	R	R
R	B	B	B
R	B	QH	R
R	B	B	B

So, for you to deal the packet out in a natural order—left to right, one row below another—the cards must be set up, from the bottom of the packet, like this: B B B R, R QH B R, B B B R, R R R B.

You'll also need a marker of some sort. A mysterious-looking medal or a foreign coin is perfect. Any coin will do, however. Hand the coin to a spectator, saying, "This will aid us in an experiment to determine whether our minds are in tune. If all works out, it might be an example of coincidence...or it might be some mysterious form of telepathy. I'll turn my back and give you some instructions. I want you to act on impulse only. Do whatever first occurs to you. If you stop to think, it could conceivably interfere with any possible telepathic waves."

Turn away and give the following instructions, pausing after each:

"Place the coin on any *red* card—complete freedom of choice."

"Move the coin to the left or the right to the nearest black card; you may choose *either* left or right. If there's no black card to the left or right, just leave the coin where it is."

"Move the coin either up or down to the nearest red card. Again, you have the choice of going *either* up or down."

"Move the coin diagonally to the nearest black card."

"Move the coin either down—toward you—or to the right to the nearest red card."

Turn back. The coin should be resting on the queen of hearts. "Let's see if we were able to mentally communicate." Turn over, in place, all of the cards except for the queen of hearts. "All blue backs." Remove the coin from the queen of hearts and turn the card over. It is, of course, the only card with a red back.

Note: The original trick is the invention of Karl Fulves.

Five Choice Cards

Alex Elmsley, one of the all-time great innovators in card magic, came up with this unique approach to a standard trick. I have made some slight changes.

Fan through the face-up deck, saying, "Let's see, we'll need five red and five black cards."

Therefore, you remove ten cards from the deck—five red, five black. You remove them one at a time, placing them into a face-up pile on the table in a particular order. The order is easy to remember. You start with a pair of alternating colors. Let's say you place a red card down face up. On top of it, you must place a black card. So face up on the table, you have: R-B.

The next four pairs will each contain a red and a black, but each will begin with the same color as the last card placed down. In this instance, the last card placed down was a black. Therefore, the next card you place down must also be a black. And it is followed by a red: R-B B-R.

The next pair? You've already guessed. It begins with a red. Thus: R-B B-R R-B.

All five pairs will be as follows: R-B B-R R-B B-R R-B. So you will either have the above order: R B B R R B B R R B. Or you will have this order: B R R B B R R B B R.

Either order will do just fine.

Pick up the pile of cards and turn it face down.

Raymond has agreed to assist you, so you must explain, "Raymond, you'll choose five of these cards." Take off the top card. "If you choose this card, it goes onto the table." Deal it onto the table, but keep your grip on it.

Replace it on top of the packet, still retaining your grip.

"If you don't choose the top card, it goes on the bottom."

Move the card to the bottom, and then back to the top.

"Let's mix the cards up a bit so that neither of us knows which is where." You're about to give the packet an up-and-down shuffle. Start by holding the cards in the left hand in the dealing position. With the left thumb, push off the top card and take it into your right hand. Move your right hand forward (away from you) a few inches and push off the next card; take it below the first one. You're now holding two cards. The top one extends about half its length beyond the lower card.

Move the right hand back to its original position and take the third card below the other two; it should be more or less in line with the first card. Move the right hand forward again, taking the fourth card below the others; it should be more or less in line with the second card. Continue through the packet.

When you're finished, hold the upper group with your left hand, as with your right hand you strip out the lower group from the others. This group goes either on top or below the cards remaining in your hand. Also, in the first move of the shuffle you may move the top card down or toward you, the next card up, the next card down, and so forth.

It's time now to ask Raymond, "Should the first card go up or go down?" Do as he indicates; then complete the up-and-down portion of the shuffle. Strip out the lower packet. "Should this packet go on top of the other packet or below it?" Do as he indicates.

Place the packet onto the table. "You'd better give them a cut, Raymond." The cards are given as many complete cuts as desired.

Pick up the packet, saying, "I'd better mix them some more." Give the packet another up-and-down shuffle, giving Raymond the same choices as before.

It seems impossible, but the top five cards are all of the same color, and, of course, so are the bottom five cards.

Put the cards behind your back. Bring the top one forward, holding it face down. "Raymond, do you want this one or not?" If he wants it, place it onto the table (or on his hand). In the latter instance, say, "Don't peek."

If the card is rejected, place it back on top. Fiddle around a bit and bring out the same card. (Presumably, you've placed it on the bottom.)

Continue like this until Raymond has chosen five cards.

"Every once in a blue moon, Raymond, a spectator proves that he has exceptional ESP by choosing cards that are all the same color. You bring the other cards forward. And, of course, you have all of the other color."

Further Thoughts

• *You might do the trick this way. Sneak a peek at the bottom card of the packet after you perform the last up-and-down shuffle. The bottom five cards will be of the same color. Ask Raymond, "Which do you prefer, Raymond—red or black?" Suppose he says red. If the bottom card was red, you let him choose from the bottom five cards. If it was black, you let him choose from the top five cards. At the end, express surprise at his ability to choose the exact color that he wanted.*

• *How do you end up with the blacks and reds separated? Simple, really. After the first up-and-down shuffle, the colors alternate. The complete cuts do not affect this order. And the next up-and-down shuffle separates the blacks and reds.*

• *The cards cannot be cut before you make your first up-and-down shuffle. This will destroy the proper order.*

TELEPHONE

Something to Sniff At

As far as I know, the original telephone trick was called *The Wizard*. Spread out the cards face up and have someone push out a card. Then dial "The Wizard," actually a confederate. When your friend answers the phone, ask, "Is The Wizard there?" Immediately the confederate begins naming the suits. Upon hearing the correct suit, you say, "Hello." Your confederate now knows the suit of the chosen card. She immediately begins naming the values, like this, "Ace, king, queen, jack, ten," etc. When she names the proper value, say, "Here," and hand the phone to the person who chose the card. The Wizard immediately tells him the name of his card.

Here we have an extremely subtle adaptation of the same trick. Again, the deck is spread out face up and a spectator pushes out a card. Dial the number of your confederate. When she answers, clear your throat. As before, she begins naming the suits. When she hits the correct suit, you sniff. She names the values. When she hits the right value, you again sniff.

Hand the phone to the spectator. Whisper to him, "Ask for your card any way you want to." When the spectator says "Hello," your confederate says, "Hello, hello. Who's calling, please? Hello." This, of course, creates the illusion that she's just answered the phone.

The spectator asks for the name of his card and is given the correct answer.

List to One Side

Time is hanging heavy on your hands. Why not telephone Nola and perform a card trick for her?

All you need is a pencil and paper, along with enough persuasive power to convince Nola to cooperate.

Start by asking her to get a deck of cards. When she returns to the phone, ask her to shuffle the deck. Then: "Nola, deal the cards from the top of the deck into a face-up pile. Please name the cards as you deal them out."

As she names the cards, jot down the name of each one, using this conventional shorthand:

9C 10S JH QD

(These stand for nine of clubs, ten of spades, jack of hearts, and queen of diamonds.)

After Nola deals ten-plus cards, tell her that she can stop whenever she wishes. Have her set the deck aside. "Pick out any card you want from those you dealt off. Remember that card and stick it into the middle of the main deck. Now shuffle up the main deck."

When she's ready, say, "Shuffle up the rest of the cards that you dealt off and put them on top of the main deck. When you're ready, give the deck a complete cut."

These are your final instructions. "Again, would you deal the cards from the top into a face-up pile and name the cards as you deal them." As she names the cards, keep your eye on the card names you jotted down. As soon as she names one, put a check mark by it. Continue checking off cards from the group. (Because she shuffled these cards, they will not be in order. But the checked-off cards *will* be together in a bunch.) Eventually, you will check off all the cards in the group except one. That is her chosen card. Stop Nola and tell her the name of her chosen card.

Sometimes the spectator will name a card from the group you wrote down but then will name cards that are not in the group. That first card she named from the group is her chosen card.

Note: When Nola names the cards for the second time, you might want to make a second list which you can use after she gets well down in the deck. This eliminates the possibility of your failing to check off one of the cards on your initial list.

GENERAL

Easy Estimation

Tricks don't get much better than this one. Apparently you can gauge the precise number of cards a spectator cuts.

Have the deck shuffled and set down. Tell a spectator to cut off a packet of cards, not too large. Then you cut off a packet, making sure it contains several more cards than the spectator's pile. Turn your back, saying, "We'll each count our cards. Then I'll tell you exactly how many you have."

With your back turned to the spectator, count your cards as he counts his. Suppose you have twenty-two. Can you make a trick out of telling the spectator that you have twenty-two cards? It doesn't seem likely, does it? Yet that is, in effect, exactly what you do.

When you turn back to the spectator, say, "I have the same number you have, three left over, and enough more to make your pile total nineteen." Repeat the statement to make sure it sinks in.

"Now let's count our cards together." As he counts his cards into a pile, you simultaneously count yours into a separate pile. The cards should be counted deliberately, and you should count out loud.

Let us suppose he has thirteen cards. You stop dealing at the same time as he does. "Thirteen," you say. "The same number you have. And I said, three left over." Deal three cards from your pile to one side, counting aloud. "Three left over. And I said that I had enough left over to make your pile total nineteen." Point to his pile. "You have thirteen." *Count now on his pile.* "Fourteen, fifteen, sixteen, seventeen, eighteen, nineteen." You were exactly right.

So far as I know, this is the only trick based solely on the use of words. As I indicated, what you *really* said to the spectator was, "I counted my cards, and it turned out I had twenty-two."

Let's try another form: "I have the same number you have and enough more to make a total of twenty-two." Wouldn't fool many people, would it?

Try this: "I have twenty-two cards, but I decided to subtract three from it, giving nineteen."

Still not tricky enough? Here's the actual form again: "I have the same number you have, three left over, and enough more to make your pile total nineteen."

You could also say, "I have the same number you have, two left over, and enough more to make your pile total twenty."

What you do, of course, is subtract a small number—two, three, or four—from your total number of cards. In the example, you counted twenty-two cards. Supposing that instead of three you decide that four should be the number left over. You subtract four from twenty-two, giving you eighteen. You now have two critical numbers, and you say, "I have the same number you have, four left over, and enough more to make your pile total eighteen." Note that these statements will work when you have a pile containing several more cards than the spectator's.

The trick can be repeated with no danger of spectators' discovering the secret. To throw them off the track, use different numbers—two, three, four—for the number of cards left over.

Let's make sure you have it. The spectator cuts off a packet. Make sure it's no more than twenty cards. Cut off a pile containing several more cards than his. Turn away, telling the spectator to count his cards while you count yours. Suppose you have twenty-five. You will choose a small number—two, three, or four—to subtract from it. Let's say you choose two. You subtract two from twenty-five, giving you twenty-three. When you turn back, you state, "I have the same number you have, two left over, and enough more to make your pile total twenty-three." Then complete the trick as described above.

There are two things that throw the spectators off: the few extra cards that you count off, and the completion of the count, not on your pile, *but on the spectator's pile.*

A Simple Swindle

This quick mental trick is a total swindle. Despite its simplicity, it never fails to fool.

Ask a spectator to shuffle the deck. If, as he does so, you're fortunate enough to catch a glimpse of the bottom card, take the deck back immediately. If not, you might learn the name of the bottom card using one of the methods given in *The Hindu Shuffle Force* (explained in *Am I Blue?*, page 26). In any instance, you must know the bottom card.

Ask the spectator to give you a number from ten to twenty. Deliberately count the cards into a pile on the table. When you come to the card at the spectator's number, deal it face down near the spectator and ask him to turn it over. As he does so, transfer the remaining cards from your left hand to your right, taking them palm down. Casually set them on top of the pile you dealt on the table. *Leave the cards there.*

Suppose the spectator gives you the number 13. Deal off 12 cards and deal the thirteenth in front of the spectator. Drop the remaining cards on top of the pile on the table as he turns the card over. It is, say, the queen of clubs. "So," you say, "the queen of clubs is the thirteenth card from the top. Easy enough. We just look at it. But what do you suppose is the thirteenth card from the bottom?"

With great effort, you arrive at the name of the card you peeked at on the bottom of the deck. Suppose it was the nine of hearts. You might say, "Queen of clubs is a black card. So the other is probably red. A heart, I would say." Concentrate. "It can't be a face card, but it's probably fairly high. An odd card, I think. A nine. Yes. The nine of hearts."

Have the spectator pick up the deck, turn it face up, and count off 13 cards. The thirteenth is the one you foretold.

Jacks Be Nimble

Start by taking the jack of hearts and the jack of spades from the deck and tossing them face up on the table. "Here we have the one-eyed jacks, and they have most peculiar properties, as you will see."

Remove a card from the deck and, without showing its face, place it on top of one of the face-up jacks, and place the other face-up jack on top of both. Explain: "Place a card between the jacks, and what do we have? Right. A one-eyed-jack sandwich."

Spread the deck for the selection of a card. Tell the spectator to look at his card and set it down for a moment. Pick up the jack sandwich and place it on top of the deck, saying, "Let's get rid of the jack sandwich." Give the cards a complete cut.

"Yes, we really do have the jack sandwich in the middle." Fan through the cards to show the jack sandwich. As you close up the deck, obtain a break below the uppermost jack with the little finger of your left hand. Transfer the break to your right thumb and perform *The Double-Cut* (see page 15).

You now have a face-up jack on the bottom, an indifferent card face down on top, and a face-up jack second from the top. Place the deck on top of the spectator's card, saying, "Did everyone see the selected card? No?"

Pick up the deck and turn it over, holding it face up in your left hand. As you display the chosen card, name it. "Now," you say to your volunteer, "I want you to pick the exact point at which I should cut the deck."

This is where you get rid of that extra card on top, the one nearest your left palm. Tilt the deck downward and then carefully draw the card away with your right hand. Your best bet is to hold the deck high in your left hand at the tips of fingers and thumb, and carefully draw the card *away from* you (Illus. a). Hand it to the spectator. "Stick it partway into the deck, anywhere you want."

Wherever he sticks the card, meticulously cut the face-up cards so that his inserted card becomes the card on the face of the deck. Straighten up the cards and set the deck on the table face down.

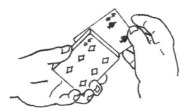

Illus. a. Hold the deck high in your left hand at the tips of fingers and thumb, and carefully draw the card away from you.

"In the deck we have your chosen card and jack sandwich. Let's take a look and see if the card in the jack sandwich can tell us anything about your card."

Fan through the face-down cards and remove the jack sandwich. Turn it over, showing the selected card between the jacks. "See how smart I was? I picked *your* card to put into the jack sandwich."

One in Four

Remove from the deck the four, three, two, and ace of any suit. (Let's assume that you're using diamonds.) First find the four and place it face up on the table. On top of this, place the face-up three, followed by the two and the ace.

Ask Jeannine to choose a card and show it around. When she returns it to the deck, bring it on the top. (See *The Double-Cut*, page 15.)

Hold the deck in the dealing position in your left hand. Pick up the four face-up cards from the table and drop them face up on top of the deck. Spread them out, along with another card or two. Say, "Here we have the ace, two, three, and four of diamonds." As you close up the four of diamonds with your palm-up right hand, get a break with your left little finger below the fifth card. Immediately, turn your right hand palm down and lift off the packet of five cards, fingers at the outer end, thumb at the inner end. The top, face-up card of the packet is the ace of diamonds, followed by the other three diamonds in order. On the bottom of the packet is the face-down chosen card.

"It's important that you remember the order of the cards," you say. "First, we have the ace." You now turn over the ace lengthwise and add it to the bottom of the packet. Here's precisely how: Move the packet in your right hand over the deck and hold down the ace with your left thumb as you move the rest of the packet to the right, drawing off the ace. The ace should extend over the right side of the deck about half its width (Illus. a). From below, lift the packet in your right hand so that its left edge flips the ace over sideways. *Leave your left thumb in place, so that the ace falls on it.* Bring your left hand over the face-down ace, so that the ace is added to the bottom of the packet.

Illus. a.

Call attention to the two of diamonds, saying, "And here we have the two." In the same way as you did the ace, turn the two of diamonds face down and add it to the bottom of the packet.

In exactly the same way, show the three and then the four. Drop the packet on top of the deck.

On top of the deck is the chosen card, followed by the ace, two, three, and four of diamonds.

Say to Jeannine, "I'd like you to choose one of the four cards—ace, two, three, or four. In fact, think of one, and then change your mind. I want you to have complete freedom of choice." She chooses one of the cards.

Suppose the ace is chosen. Deal the top card face down onto the table, saying, "All right, there's the ace. Now let's see how the two behaves." Without showing the top card, place it second from the top. Tap the top card and then turn it over. Apparently the two has returned to the top. Place the two *face up* next to the card on the table.

"Let's check the three." Place the top card second from the top. Tap the top card and turn it over. The three has returned. Deal it face up next to the two.

"And the four?" Again, place the top card second from the top. Tap the top card and turn it over, showing that the four has returned. Deal it face up to the right of the three.

Gesture toward the table. "So we have ace, two, three, and four of diamonds. And you chose the ace. What's the name of your card?" The spectator names it. Turn over the face-down card. Success!

Suppose the spectator chooses two, three, or four. In each instance, the chosen number is simply dealt face down onto the table; each of the others is placed second from the top, brought back to the top, turned face up, and dealt face up onto the table.

Let's suppose Jeannine chooses three, for instance. "Fine," you say. "Let's see how the ace behaves." Place the top card second from the top. Tap the top card, showing that the ace has returned. Place the ace on the table face up.

Place the top card second from the top, saying, "Let's see what the two does." Tap the top card. Sure enough, the two has returned to the top. Deal it face up to the right of the ace. Deal the next card face down to the right of the other two cards, saying. "Here's your three."

Once more place the top card second from the top, saying, "Let's see what the four does." Tap the top card; the four has returned to the top. Deal it face up to the right of the other three cards.

In all instances, you finally ask the name of the chosen card and then turn it face up.

Note: This trick is quite similar to the previous trick in its basic principle. But its effect is quite different. Roy Walton combined tricks by Al Baker and Dai Vernon; my only contribution is to add a slightly different handling.

Good Choice

Here's a fast, clever trick requiring only nerve and a bit of practice.

In your pocket, you have four kings. The king of spades and the king of clubs have blue backs. The king of hearts and the king of diamonds have red backs. The order doesn't matter.

Remove the four cards from your pocket, making sure spectators cannot see any of the backs. Hold them face up in your left hand. Spread the kings out and ask Ted to name one (Illus.

a). After he does so, say, "You can change your mind if you want to, Ted—it doesn't matter." When he finally decides on one, remove it from the group, saying, "This one." Replace it so it's the lowermost of the face-up cards. Maneuver the other cards about so the king of the same color as the one chosen is at the face of the packet. As you do this, say, "You could have chosen this one, or this one, whatever one you wished." Tell him that he can still change his mind. If he does, maneuver the cards so they're in the appropriate position described.

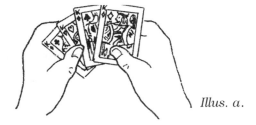

Illus. a.

You are about to perform a variation of the *flushtration count*, the invention of Brother John Hamman. Close up the face-up packet and hold it from above in your right hand, fingers at the outer end and thumb at the inner end. Turn your right hand palm up, displaying the back of the top, chosen card. Let's assume Ted has selected the king of clubs. Say, "It's amazing that you should choose the king of clubs, which has a *blue* back." Turn your right hand palm down. With the left *fingers*, draw the king of clubs from the back of the packet into your left hand. (This first maneuver differs from the standard *flushtration count*.) Turn your right hand palm down and, with your left thumb, draw off the card at the face of the packet so that it comes to rest on top of the king of clubs. (This is the standard move in the *flushtration count.*) Perform the action again. Then display the back of the last card, turn your right hand palm down and drop the card face up on top of those in your left hand.

Ted has chosen the only card with a different-colored back.

Further Thoughts

If you wish, repeat the trick several times. Simply put the cards into your pocket. Chat for a moment about what a coincidence has occurred. Then say, "I have another set of kings in my pocket." Dig into a different pocket. "No luck. Maybe they're here." Take the same set of kings from your pocket and repeat the trick. You might even put the kings away again and then go through the same routine. The basic trick is so deceptive that there's little danger that spectators will catch on, and it becomes quite amusing when spectators suspect that you're using the same kings.

Wedded Bliss

Remove from the deck all the kings and queens as you chat about how important a good marriage is. "Here," for instance, "we have four loving, loyal couples." Without calling attention to the suits, lay the eight cards out like this (your view):

KC   QC   KH   QH
KS   QS   KD   QD

Note that in the top row you have the club marriage, followed by the heart marriage. In the second row you have the spade marriage, followed by the diamond marriage. (In other words, the couples are in CHaSeD order.)

Gesture toward the layout. "Just look at those happy couples!" Turn all the cards face down in place. "No matter how you split them up, they always want to be back together." Exchange the fourth card in the top row with the third card in the second row; exchange the second card in the top row with the first card in the second row. (In other words, exchange the QH and KD, and then the QC and KS.) The layout now (with the cards face down):

KC	KS	KH	KD
QC	QS	QH	QD

Ask Myrna to assist you. Turn the KH face up, saying, "Here we have a happy king. Myrna, do you think you can find his mate, the QH?" Surprisingly, hardly anyone can pick out the QH on the first try, and very seldom on the second try.

If Myrna should get it on her first attempt, compliment her on how observant she is. If she misses, show the card she chose and turn it face down again. "I'll give you another chance, Myrna." If she gets it, praise her as before. But if not, show the card she chose and turn it face down. "Now Myrna, I wish you'd stop fooling around. Which one is the QH?"

If she misses as many as four times, I usually tap the QH and ask, "Have you tried this one yet?" When she finally gets it, turn the card face up and offer congratulations. Set aside the KH and QH face up, fanned out (Illus. a).

Gather the remaining cards one on top of the other in their natural order:

1	2	3
4	5	6

Illus. a.

Or you may gather them up in reverse order—either way will work.

Have Myrna give the packet as many complete cuts as she wants. "Now, without looking at it, please place the top card face down right next to the king and queen of hearts."

After she's done this, continue (with appropriate pauses): "Place the top card on the bottom, and put the next card down in front of you. Place the next card on the bottom, and place the next card on top of the one you just put down. Place the next card on the bottom, and place the next card on the pile."

When she gets down to one card, say, "Place the next card on the bottom. Whoops! That's going to be really hard to do." Pause. "You set aside one card. Let's see if we have a match."

Yes. The card she's holding is the loving mate to the one she set aside. These two are turned face up and are placed, fanned out, next to the king and queen of hearts.

"Let's try again. Without looking at it, place the top card face down by the face-up couples. Now place the top card on the bottom, and put the next card..."

Myrna's last card is shown to match the one she set aside. These two are displayed with the others, fanned out. And the two dealt to the table are turned over and added to the display.

Don't neglect the display! It makes a colorful, satisfying conclusion.

Note: This is Werner Miller's clever concoction; I've made the trick more amusing and have changed the ending.

Shifting Faces

My version requires no sleights.

"I need nine face cards," you say as you fan through the cards, faces toward you. Cut a king to the top. As far as the audience knows, you've just cut a face card to the bottom. Fan through to find another king. Separate the card at that point and slip the king to the bottom. All of this is done quite openly.

In the same way, slip a queen to the bottom, and then a jack. Continue until you have the following eight cards on the bottom, the last one being the bottom card: K Q J J K Q Q J. (The suits are irrelevant.) Think of the order as two sequences of K Q J. In the first sequence, you double the jack; in the second, you double the queen.

Take the bottom eight cards off the deck, faces toward you. Casually show the bottom card of the deck. Set the deck face down. You've already said that you need nine face cards, so there's no need to mention the number.

Fan out the top three cards, take them off the packet, and show them to a spectator. "King, queen, jack. Right?" Right. Place the three on the bottom of the packet. In the same way, show the next three to another spectator, repeating your comment. Also place these on the bottom. Repeat the procedure with a third spectator. Actually, one of the cards you showed the first spectator is in the group shown to the third spectator.

(Incidentally, you can show the trick to just one person. I've never had anyone note that a card in the third group has already been shown.)

Drop the packet on top of the deck. Time for a pause. Say, "So we have three groups, with a king, queen, and jack in each group. Even I can figure that out." Fan out the top three cards, take them off the deck, and place them on the table. Say, "Three." Fan off three more and place them on the others, saying, "Three more." Do it once more, saying, "And three more."

Pick up the packet and take off the top card, a jack, and drop it face up on the table. Point to it, saying, "This is the card that makes it all work." Pick up the jack and slap it against the packet several times, saying whatever magical words occur to you. Place the jack, still face up, on the bottom of the packet.

One by one, deal the top three cards (the kings) face up, overlapping them. Next to them deal the next three cards (the queens) face up. And next to the queens, deal the jacks face up. The last jack, of course, is already face up.

Lucky 13

As I was playing around with the cards one day, a new concept occurred to me. It took me a while to put a trick to it. What I finally developed has provided me, and spectators, with a lot of fun.

Reuben agrees to assist you. Say to him, "Most people believe that the number 13 is bad luck. But for me, it's always been good luck. Let me demonstrate. Reuben, I'm going to show you 13 cards. But first, I want you to think of a number from 1 to 13—not too high and not too low. Do you have one? Okay. Now I'd like you to notice what card lies at that number. Please don't stop me until we've done all 13 cards."

Take off the top card and show it to Reuben, saying "One." Drop the card face down onto the table. Show the second card, saying "Two." Drop this card face down onto the first card. Continue through 13 cards. Set the deck aside for the moment.

"Do you have your card? Good. Let me see if I can figure out what it is." Concentrate briefly. "No, it isn't coming to me. Maybe it'll help if you tell me the number you thought of."

Let's say that Reuben says 8. "So your card is 8 from the bottom. 8 from 13 is 5." Pick up the packet. Deal off four cards into a face-down pile, reciting the numbers 1 through 4 as you do so. Lift off the next card, saying "Five." Toss the card face down onto the table, forward of the others. Drop the remaining cards in your hand on top of the cards you just dealt off. Tap the single card you tossed onto the table, saying, "I'm going to try to discover the name of your card without once looking at its face." Avert your head as you pick up the card and drop it on top of the main deck. Pick up the packet on the table and put it on top of the deck.

The chosen card is now on top of the deck. Tap the top card. "Right here is a magical card. This card will help me figure out what your card is." Lift off the card and study it, making sure no one else can see its face. Suppose the card is the three of clubs. Say hesitantly, "This tells me that your card is...black." Stall around. Eventually reveal that the card tells you that the suit is clubs. Grimace as you once more stare at the face of the card. "This magical card tells me that your card is...an eight...No!...a three. Your card is the three of clubs. Right?"

Right.

"Boy, I *love* this magical card!" Toss it onto the table face up.

Further Thoughts

This trick works because most people have never had occasion to consider the actual mathematics involved. Let's take our example with Reuben; in the pile of 13 cards, you have a particular card at the eighth position from the bottom. What is its number from the top?

To the vast majority of spectators, it seems logical to subtract 8 from 13 to get the proper number. You certainly don't provide any time to think about it. But the actual number from the top is 6, not 5. And that, of course, is the basis of this trick. Suppose the particular card is at the fifth position from the bottom: the number from the top is 9, not 8, and so on.

If someone does catch on, it doesn't matter much with this particular trick.

The Unknown Number

Oscar is willing to help, so you hand him the deck and turn away. You provide these directions with appropriate pauses: "Please shuffle the deck, Oscar. Cut off a fairly good-sized group of cards. (This ensures that the group will be higher than 10 and, preferably, higher than 19.) Count the cards that you just cut off.

You now have a two-digit number, right? Add these two digits together. Don't tell me your total. But count that many cards back into the deck. For instance, suppose you cut off 24 cards. You have two digits—the 2 and the 4. Add these two together, getting 6. So you'd count six cards back onto the deck."

Give Oscar some time to accomplish this. "Now push the deck to one side; we won't be using it any longer. You're still holding the rest of the cards that you cut off. From this group take some cards—say, fewer than 10—put them into your pocket."

Turn back and take the remainder of the cut-off cards from Oscar. Fan through them, letting all see the faces, as you say, "Let's see what face cards you have here." Inspect the group carefully. If there are face cards, pull them out and comment on each one. You might say, "Oh, yes, the jack of spades. Very significant." If there are no face cards, you could say, "Just as I thought—no face cards." Actually, you count the cards. Reduce the total to a single digit. For instance, if you count 13 cards, add the 1 and the 3, getting 4. Subtract the single digit from 9. This gives you the number of cards that Oscar has in his pocket.

In our example, you subtracted 4 from 9, getting 5. You announce the number. But not immediately. You might say something like, "I have the king of spades, which means that you have an odd number of cards in your pocket, Oscar. And this jack of hearts indicates that it's a fairly low number. I'd say that you have five cards in your pocket."

And if there are no face cards among those you hold, you could say, "No face cards at all, Oscar. That means that you have an ordinary number of cards—probably five. Yes, I think you have five cards in your pocket."

Further Thoughts

• *The trick will work when the spectator cuts off any number of cards from 10 to 51.*

• *Suppose you're looking through the packet, presumably looking for face cards, but actually counting, and you find that the packet contains 18 cards. You add 1 and 8, getting 9. You subtract 9 from 9, getting 0. This means that the spectator has nine cards in his pocket. It's possible that a smart aleck might put no cards in his pocket. I've never had this occur, but if it did, I would first announce that he had nine cards in his pocket. If he said no, I'd tell him he had zero cards in his pocket. And perhaps make a sarcastic comment about his choice.*

Note: This is an updated version of a trick I invented many decades ago.

Double Dealing

So-called "self-working" card tricks are plentiful, but are sometimes tedious or unremarkable, or both. Rarely does one come along that's clever, interesting, and deceptive. Here we have one, however. I have no idea who invented it, but it was called to my attention by my friend Wally Wilson. I have added a minor touch.

You'll need three coins: a dime, a quarter, and a half-dollar. In presentation, you can probably borrow a dime and a quarter, but not too many people carry a half-dollar. So when you plan to perform the trick, you should probably have a half-dollar available. (In the *Notes* at the end, I'll explain how you can perform the trick without using American coins.)

Ask Janet to assist you. Place the three coins onto the table, saying, "Janet, we're going to use these in a moment to test your psychic ability. Sometimes an astonishing coincidence occurs, and, of course, sometimes it doesn't."

Go through the deck and find a 2. Place this face up onto the table. On top of it place another 2 of any other suit. On top of this place a pair of face-up fours of any suits. These are followed by pairs of sixes, eights, tens, and queens. There are six pairs in all. From the face down, here is the layout:

Q Q 10 10 8 8 6 6 4 4 2 2

Make no attempt to hide the fact that each pair consists of matching values, but don't call attention to it either. Actually, the six pairs could be of any different values; this method, raising the value by two each time, guarantees that you won't accidentally have two pairs of the same value.

Set the rest of the deck aside. Pick up the pile of pairs, saying, "I'd better mix them up a bit."

You now perform an up-and-down shuffle. In the first move, your right hand takes the top cards and moves forward a few inches. The next card goes below the first one and extends *toward* you. Continue alternating like this through the packet. Strip out the lower group and set these cards on top of those remaining in your left hand. Set the packet onto the table. Turn it face down.

"Janet, please give the cards a cut. And you may cut the cards as many more times as you wish."

Her complete cuts do not change the basic order. So the up-

and-down shuffle has arranged the cards so that the top six cards are in the same order as the bottom six. (Be sure to perform the up-and-down shuffle *before* the packet is cut; otherwise, this vital setup could be ruined.)

The cards now might look like this, from the face to the top:

6 8 10 Q 2 4 6 8 10 Q 2 4

The cards could actually be set up like this at the beginning, but I prefer my method, which creates the illusion that the cards are thoroughly mixed. At this point, you might ask another spectator to give the packet a cut or two.

Pick up the packet and do the following:

1. Deal a face-down row of three cards, going from left to right.

2. Below that, deal another face-down row of three cards, again going from left to right.

3. Deal one face-down card on top of each card in that second row, going from left to right.

4. Repeat step 3. (See Illus. a for the present position, from your point of view.)

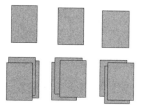

Illus. a.

Say to Janet, "Please pick up the three coins and distribute them so that one is on top of each one of these cards." Indicate the first row of cards you dealt.

Note the coin that rests on the card on your left. Let's say that it's the quarter. Call Janet's attention to it. Pick up the three-card pile on your left. "Janet, you placed the quarter on the card above this pile. I'll spell the word *quarter*, moving one card from the top to the bottom of this pile for each letter." Do so. Then take the card which is now on top of the pile and place it on top of the coin whose name you just spelled. The quarter now rests on a card and has another card on top of it. "As you can see, Janet, we now have a sort of coin sandwich."

You pick up the middle pile of three cards and, in the same way as above, spell out the name of the coin above it. Place the top card of this pile on top of the coin you just spelled.

Do the same with the last pile.

"Don't forget, Janet: You cut the cards a number of times, and you had complete freedom of choice as to where to put the coins. Now let's see how you did."

Turn the two cards over that surround the first coin. The cards are of the same value. Do the same with the cards that surround the second coin. And, of course, repeat with the cards that surround the third coin.

For most, this will seem an excellent trick, so pause a moment to let it sink in. Then: "I thought that was an amazing coincidence, Janet, but I can see that you're not too impressed. Let's see if there are any more coincidences."

Turn each of the remaining pairs face up. That is, turn over each pair that remains in the second row. Each pair consists of two cards of the same value.

"Now *there's* a coincidence!"

Further Thoughts

• *Why does the trick work? When you spell out the value of the coin in your three-card pile, you want to end up with the top card being the original second card from the top. This will happen when the spelling consists of four letters* (dime), *seven letters* (quarter), *or ten letters* (half-dollar). *Obviously, you just keep adding three, so the spelling would work out with words consisting of 13 letters, 16, 19, 22, etc. It's amazingly ingenious, I believe, that the inventor took advantage of the various spellings to fashion this astounding trick.*

• *You can readily work the trick without using American coins. You must find small objects which spell out with four letters, seven letters, and ten letters, respectively.*

The theme could be snacks, for instance. Four-letter objects could be soda *or* cola (a can); *seven-letter ones could be* pretzel, popcorn, *or* cracker; *and a ten-letter one could be* potato chip.

Many possibilities are available when you use no particular theme. Four-letter objects could be ring, comb, book, *or* fork; *seven-letter objects could be* key ring *or* glasses; *ten-letter objects could be* spectacles, wristwatch, *or* tiny bottle.

Undoubtedly, many other possibilities will occur to you.

AN OUT

The spectator names his selected card; you turn over the one in your hand, and it's the wrong one. Here's a way out.

Show the card and return it to the deck, asking, "Are you sure the five of spades was your card?" Fan through the cards so that no one else can see the faces. "It must be here somewhere."

What you want to do is bring the chosen card second from the top. Fan several cards from the bottom and transfer them to the top in a bunch. Continue doing this until you come to the chosen card. Fan one card beyond it and put that group on top. Confess, "No luck."

Turn the deck face down in the dealing position in your left hand. Take the top card and turn it face up. As you do so, push off the second card (the chosen one) slightly with your left thumb and then draw it back, taking a slight break under it with your left little finger.

Immediately place the card in your right hand face up on the deck. Square the ends of the deck with your right fingers and thumb. The two cards are now as one, separated slightly from the rest of the deck by the tip of your little finger.

"Obviously your card isn't on top." Grasp the double card with your right hand from above, thumb at the rear, second finger at the front, and first finger resting on top. Dig your left thumb beneath the deck and flip the deck face up. Place the double card underneath, presumably replacing on top the card you've just shown (Illus. a). Carefully even up the deck, saying, "And equally obviously, your card isn't on the bottom. Watch for your card."

Illus. a.

Fan ten or so cards from the bottom. "It's not among these." Turn these cards face down and put them on the back of the deck (Illus. b). Continue this way all through the deck. The last group you take includes all the cards up to the first face-down card. Presumably, you've shown every card in the deck, and the chosen card isn't among them. Actually, it's at

Illus. b.

your disposal on top of the deck.

How do you reveal it? You might do *Sneaky Slide* (page 22), in which you double-lift the top card, showing that the chosen card is still not there. Then you lift off the top card, slide it through the deck edgewise, and turn it over, showing that it has changed to the chosen card.

A second possibility is one which is also a good trick on its own merits. Put the deck into your pocket. Remove a card from the bottom and place it on the table. *Rapidly* continue doing this, saying, "Tell me when to stop." Make sure you get your hand back to your pocket when the spectator says stop, so that you can pull out the top card and flip it over face up.

CARD GAMES

BEFORE YOU BEGIN

Solitaire is really the ultimate game—one in which it is very clear that you are competing only against yourself and the run of the cards (sort of like life?). Win or not, we hope you enjoy playing the games!

There are a few terms you need to be familiar with:

• *Suit*   There are four of them: hearts, diamonds, clubs, and spades.

• *Suite*—A full set of thirteen cards of one suit: ace to king of clubs, for example.

• *To build*—To place one card on another to create a sequence—whatever kind is called for. Usually the sequence just goes up or down—the queen, for example, is placed on the king if the sequence is down, on the jack if it's up.

• *Building upward in suit* means laying down cards from low to high—from the ace (or wherever you have to start from)—to the king (or wherever you have to end at)—in one single suit: from the ace to the king of hearts, for instance.

• *Building downward in suit* means laying down cards from high to low—from the king of hearts through the ranks to the ace, for example.

• *Rank*—The card's number. A ten of diamonds "ranks" higher than a nine of diamonds.

• *Foundations*—The cards that score—the ones you build

on. They are usually put up above the layout, as in the most popular solitaire games, *Klondike* and *Canfield*. But sometimes they are placed differently—or not placed at all.

• *The stockpile*—The cards that are left in your hand after you have completed the layout.

• *The wastepile*—The collection of discarded cards.

• *A column*—Cards that go vertically in a line.

• *A row*—Cards that go horizontally in a line.

• *Deuces*—Twos.

SOLITAIRE GAMES

Accordion

Other Names: Idle Year, Tower of Babel, Methuselah
Space: Small/Moderate
Level: Difficult
Play: Start by dealing the cards one at a time face up in a row of four from left to right. Go slowly so that you can keep comparing the cards you deal with their neighbors. Whenever a card matches the card on its left—or third to the left—you move the new card over onto the one it matches. The match may be in suit or rank.

Let's say that the first four cards you turn up are:

The eight of spades matches the eight of clubs (on its left) and also the five of spades (third to the left). You could move it onto either one. Which one will turn out better? You really can't tell at this point.

Once you move a card over; though, the card on the bottom doesn't have any more significance. The card on top is the one to match.

As soon as you move a card—or a pile—move the later cards over to close up the sequence. That will open up new moves for you, too.

Go on dealing cards, one at a time, stopping after each one to make whatever moves are possible, until you've used up all the cards.

For example, suppose that you deal:

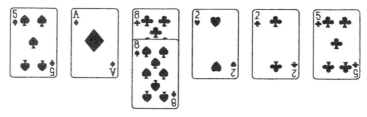

You can move the two of clubs onto the two of hearts. Then close up the row. The five of clubs moves next to the twos. It's a club, and that's a match! But once you move the five over onto the two of clubs, another move opens up: You can move the entire pile over onto the five of spades, which is the third card to the left. So the cards look like the illustration on the following page.

To win the game: Get the whole pack into one pile. It's almost impossible. If you end up with five piles, you're doing pretty well.

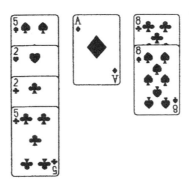

Aces Up

Other Names: Idiot's Delight, Firing Squad
Space: Small
Level: Moderate
Layout: Deal four cards in a row.
Play: If you have two cards of the same suit, discard the one that is lower in rank. Aces are high. For example, here you have:

Discard the five of hearts.

When you've made all the moves you can, fill the empty space in the row with any top card from the layout. In this case, where there is only one layer of cards as yet, fill the space from

the cards in your hand. Then deal four more cards overlapping
the ones you've already set up.

Go through the same process of discarding the lower card of
the same suit from the new layer of cards.

And so on until you've gone through the whole pack.

To win the game: Discard all the cards—except the aces, of
course.

Baker's Dozen

Other Names: None
Space: Wide
Level: Easy
Layout: Deal 13 columns of four overlapping cards. Aces will
go into a foundation row above the layout.

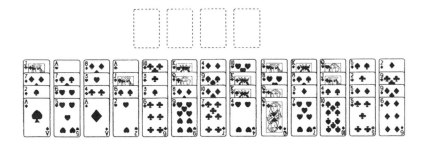

After you lay out the cards, check on the kings. If a king is
in an exposed position, move it underneath the other cards in
the column. If a king is lying on another card of the same suit,
place it underneath that card.

To win the game: Release aces and build them up to kings in suit.

Play: Build downward on the cards in the layout, one card at a time, regardless of color or suit. Do not fill any spaces.

Perseverance

Level: Moderate

Play exactly the same way as *Baker's Dozen*, except:

1. Set aces in foundation piles from the start.

2. Lay out twelve columns of four overlapping cards each.

3. If a group of cards is in suit and in sequence, starting at the top, you can move the entire sequence as a unit.

4. On the layout, build down in suit only.

5. You have two redeals. Gather up the piles in the reverse order of the way you put them down, and then deal them back into twelve columns, as far as they go.

Good Measure

Play exactly the same way as *Baker's Dozen*, except:

1. Deal ten columns of five overlapping cards.

2. Start with two aces in the foundation row.

Canfield

Other Names: Fascination, Thirteen, Demon
Space: Small
Level: Difficult

Canfield is one of the most popular solitaire games in the world. A shorter, faster game than *Klondike, Canfield* is played much the same way, but it starts from a different basic layout.

Canfield came by its name in an interesting way. Mr. Canfield owned a gambling house in Saratoga Springs in the 1890s. He used to sell his customers packs of cards at $50 each and then pay them back $5 for every card they were able to score. Estimates are that the average number of cards you could expect to score in a game was five or six, so Mr. Canfield did pretty well.

Layout: Count out 13 cards into one pile and put it in front of you face up and a little to your left. Then put a 14th card to the right of the pile and slightly above it; whatever that card is, it becomes the foundation card of this particular deal. As the other cards of the same rank appear, you'll be placing them too in the foundation row.

To win the game: Build the foundation cards into four complete suits of 13 cards each.

Next, you lay out a row of four cards below the foundation card, face up:

No cards are ever built on the 13-pile. The object is to unload it. For example, in the illustration above, you couldn't put a five—or any other card—on the six. Cards from the 13-pile can be played only onto the foundations or into the four-card row when a space opens up.

Play: First check the four-card spread carefully to see whether you can make any moves. Besides playing cards to the foundations, you can build cards onto the four-card spread downward in alternating colors.

For instance, in the illustration above, the three of hearts can go onto the four of spades; the seven of diamonds can go up into the foundation row; and the six of spades can come down into the row of four. Once it does, the five of hearts can be played onto it.

You are permitted to move sequences of cards as one unit. For example, the 3 and 4 may be moved together onto the 5 and 6, so your layout would look like this:

Then you can proceed to fill the other open spaces in the four-card row with cards from the 13-pile.

Now start turning up cards from the pack, in batches of three, playing them either to the foundations, to the four-card row, or to the wastepile. The top card of the wastepile is always available for play.

As spaces open up in the four-card row, continue to fill them with cards from the 13-card pile. When these are exhausted, you can fill them with cards from your hand or from the wastepile. **Redeal:** As many times as you want, or until the game is blocked.

The Clock

**Other Names: Hidden Cards, Sundial, Four of a
                Kind, All Fours, Travellers, Hunt**
Space: Moderate
Level: Easy
Deal the pack into 13 face-down piles of four cards each.

Arrange 12 of them in a circle, representing the numbers on a clock dial. Put the thirteenth pile in the middle of the circle. It should look like the illustration on the following page.

Start by picking up the top card of the middle pile. Suppose it's a five. Slip it, face up, under the pile of cards that are in the five-o'clock position. Then pick up the top card of the five-o'clock pile. Suppose it's a jack. It would go under the eleven-o'clock pile (remember, the king pile is in the middle of the clock—and the queen is at 12). And you would pick up the top card of the eleven-o'clock pile and slip it under whatever pile it belongs in.

When you slip the fourth card of any group into place—and

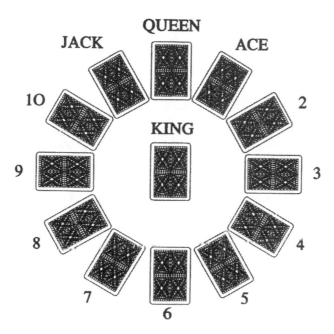

there is no face-down card to turn over—turn over the top card of the next-highest card pile.

To win the game: Get all the cards turned face up before the fourth king is turned face up.

Double or Quits

Other Names: None
Space: Small
Level: Easy

Tricky building—and on only one foundation!

Layout: Deal seven cards in a sort of frame shape, as shown below. Then place a card inside the frame. That card is the foundation, and you can build on it from the frame or from the stockpile. If any of the cards in the layout turn out to be kings, put them on the bottom of the deck and replace them with other cards.

To win the game: Build all the cards onto the foundation—except for kings—doubling the value of the card that has just been placed.

Play: For example, let's say the layout looks like this:

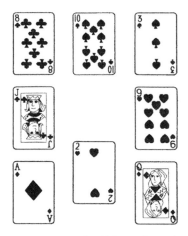

The card you've got to build on is a deuce, so you deal out the cards, one by one, until you come to a four of any suit—

and place that on the deuce. The cards that you go through before you come to the four go on the wastepile.

The next card you need to find is double 4—or an 8. There is one in the frame, so you can use that right away. Spaces in the frame are filled with the top card of the wastepile or, if there is no wastepile, from your hand.

Double 8 is 16. So deduct 13 (the number of cards in a suit) and you get 3: this is the card you need to find next.

So—a sequence goes like this and repeats:

2 4 8 3 6 queen (12) jack (11) 9 5 10 7 A 2

Redeals: Two.

Fourteens

**Other Names: Fourteen Puzzle, Fourteen Out,
                  Take Fourteen**

Space: Large

Level: Easy

Layout: Deal the cards, face up, in 12 columns of four cards each. You'll have four cards left over. Just put them on the first four columns.

Arrange the cards so that you can see them all.

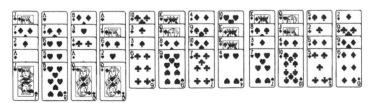

Play: Remove pairs of available cards whose totals add up to 14. There will be, of course:

ace and king	four and ten
two and queen	five and nine
three and jack	six and eight

Available cards are the ones that are exposed at the bottoms of the columns.

To win the game: You win when all cards have been discarded.

Gaps

Other Names: Spaces
Space: Large
Level: Difficult
Layout: Deal all the cards in the pack—in four rows of 13 cards, each face up.

Then remove the aces. This leaves gaps in the layout. These gaps must be filled by the card that is next higher in rank to the card on the left—and in the same suit. For example, suppose the gap opens up to the right of a three of hearts. It must be filled by a four of hearts.

If the gap opens up in the first space at the left of a row, it may be filled with any deuce.

If the gap opens up after a king, it cannot be filled. Action is blocked.

When a king blocks the action in every row, the deal is over.

To win the game: Get each row into a sequence of cards from 2 to king, by suit.

Redeals: As many as you want. You need to gather up the cards in a special way for the redeal. Leave in place the deuces that appear at the left end of a row and any cards that follow it in the correct sequence and suit. For example:

Then, gather up all the not-in-place cards, shuffle them, and deal them out as follows:

Leave these   **but not these**

1. Leave one gap to the right of each sequence.

2. If the only card in place is a two, leave a gap to the right of it.

3. If there is no two in the row, leave a gap at the start of the row, so that a two can be moved in.

Grandfather's Clock

Other Names: None
Space: Huge
Level: Easy
Layout: Remove the following cards from the deck and place them in a circle, as in the illustration below:

two of hearts	eight of diamonds
three of spades	nine of clubs
four of diamonds	ten of hearts
five of clubs	jack of spades
six of hearts	queen of diamonds
seven of spades	king of clubs

These are the foundations on which you are going to be building a "real" clock face.

Place the remaining cards in eight columns of five cards each. Overlap the cards so you can see them all.

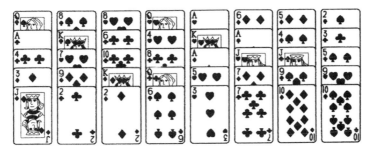

Play: Using the exposed cards in the layout, build the foundations—the cards on the clock face—up in suit until the cards on the top correspond to the numbers on a real clock face (with jack as eleven o'clock and the queen at twelve).

In order to free the cards to do this, build on the cards in the layout—downward, regardless of suit.

Spaces may be filled by any available card.

To win the game: Get the clock to have the right number values on its face, as in the illustration below:

Hit or Miss

Other Names: Treize Roll Call, Talkative, Harvest
Space: Small
Level: Very Difficult
Play: Go through the cards one by one, naming each one as you go. The first one would be "ace," the second "deuce," the eleventh "jack," and so on.

When your name and the rank of the card are the same, it's a *hit*, and you get to discard the card.

You are allowed to go through the cards as many times as you want—or until you go through the entire pack twice without a hit.

To win the game: Discard every card in the deck.

Klondike

Other Names: Canfield, Small Triangle, Fascination,
               Demon Patience, Triangle
Space: Moderate
Level: Difficult
Layout: Lay out seven cards in a row—face down except for the first card. Then put the eighth card face up on the second card in the row, and complete the row with face-down cards. Place a face-up card on the third pile, and finish off the row in the same way. Continue until you have a face-up card on every pile.

Your layout will look like the illustration on the next page.

To win the game: Build up complete suites from ace to king. Aces are low in this game.

Play: First, look over the spread carefully. Move any cards that

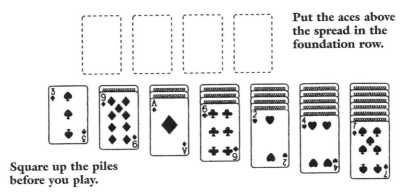

Put the aces above the spread in the foundation row.

Square up the piles before you play.

you can to the foundation row—aces and any cards you can build on them.

You can also build cards on the layout itself. Only the face-up cards are available for this building, and only if they are the exposed cards of the pile. Then you can build downward in alternating colors.

In the example shown here, you can move the ace to the foundation row, and then move the black three onto the red four, and the red two onto the black three.

Every time you move a face-up card, you need to turn up the face-down card beneath it. When there are no more face-down cards in a pile, you have a space. Spaces can be filled by any available king.

When you've made all the moves you can, start going through the stockpile one by one, looking for more cards to build onto the foundations and the layout. If you can't place the card, it goes face up onto a wastepile, and the top card of the wastepile is available for play.

Scoring: Five rounds make a game. Add up the number of foundation cards in each round for your final score.

Little Spider

Other Names: None
Space: Small
Level: Moderate
Layout: Lay out four cards face up in a row along the top of your playing space, and four cards in a row beneath them—leaving space for a row in between. That's where the foundations will go—two aces of one color and two kings of another—as they become available:

Two aces of one color

Two kings of another color

To win the game: Build the aces in suit to kings and the kings in suit to aces.

During the deal: You can move any card from the top row onto the foundations. But you cannot move a card from the bottom row unless it can be moved straight up into place—into the position directly above its original position. For example, in the illustration on the left on the facing page, the two of hearts can go on the ace of hearts, but in the picture on the right, it can't.

Play: When you've made all the moves you can to the foundations, deal another four cards to the top and bottom rows. Make your moves, and then deal again—until all the cards have been laid out.

At this point, the special rules for "During the deal" no longer apply. You can move any card from the top or bottom rows onto the foundation piles. You can also build top cards from the layout onto each other regardless of suit or color—up or down.

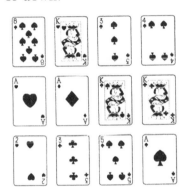

Two of hearts can go straight up onto the ace, because the ace is the same suit.

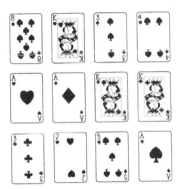

Two of hearts cannot go onto the ace, because it is not directly under the ace of hearts.

Spaces in the layout may not be filled.
Kings may be placed on aces.

Monte Carlo

Other Names: Weddings
Space: Moderate
Level: Moderate
Layout: Deal five rows of five cards each, so your layout looks like this:

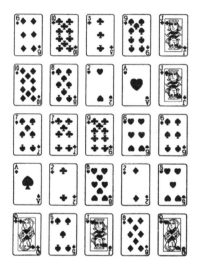

To win the game: Discard the entire deck in pairs of the same rank. You can discard them if they are:

1. Next to each other
2. Above or below each other
3. "Touching" diagonally

Play: Remove every pair that you can from the layout. When you do, there will be holes. Close up the cards so that all the holes are filled and the cards are in the same order in which you laid them out.

After you make the cards into solid rows again, deal new cards to make up the bottom rows, so that you have five rows of five cards again.

Remove the pairs again in the same way, and when you can't move any more cards, go through the process of closing up the layout spaces and filling in at the end with cards from your hand.

Poker Solitaire

Other Names: Poker Squares
Space: Moderate
Level: Moderate
Layout: Deal 25 cards in five rows of five cards each. Each row and each column is a poker hand; so, in any game, you have ten hands with which to build your total score.

SCORING	American	English
Royal Flush		
Five of the same suit in sequence starting with an ace	100	30
Straight Flush		
In sequence five of the same suit	75	30
Four of a Kind		
Four of the same rank	50	16
Full House		
Three of a kind + two of a kind	25	10
Flush		
Five of the same suit, but not in sequence	20	5

	American	English
Straight Five in sequence, but not in the same suit	15	12
Three of a Kind	10	6
Two Pairs	5	3
One Pair	2	1

To win the game: Come up with the highest score.

Play: Rearrange the cards in the layout so that you have the highest-scoring poker hand possible.

In some versions of this game, after you move a card once, you cannot move it again.

Pyramid

Other Names: Pile of 28
Space: Moderate
Level: Difficult

A sad thing about many solitaire games is that you play a round—or five rounds—and then it's over. You have no special feeling of victory (unless you've played out and won) and no standard with which to compare your score.

Here's a game that keeps you counting and scoring all the time. You can play it against yourself, against another player, or against "par."

Layout: Lay out the cards in the shape of a pyramid, starting with one card at the top and placing two cards that overlap it, then three overlapping them, and so on, until you have a large triangle with seven cards as its base.

Each card has its own numerical value (face value); kings count as 13, queens as 12, and jacks as 11.

Play: Your job is to remove pairs of cards that add up to 13, with this catch: You cannot remove a card unless it is "exposed"—not covered by any other card.

For example, in the pyramid above, you can remove the 7 and the 6 from the bottom row. This opens up the ace in the row above, which you can remove with the queen (worth 12) in the bottom row.

You can remove kings alone, because they add up to 13 without any help.

Place all the cards you remove in a special "Removed" pile, face up. The top card in this pile can be used again to form another 13-match.

Now you start dealing out the rest of the pack, one by one. If the card you turn up does not form a match with an available card in the pyramid, put it into a wastepile. Don't mix up this pile with your "Removed" pile.

If one of the cards you turn up from your hand is a match with the top card of the "Removal" pile, you can remove both of them.

To win the game: You need to remove the entire pyramid plus the cards in your hand.

Redeals: Two.

How to score pyramid: A match is six games. Score each game as follows:

50 points—If you get rid of your pyramid in the first deal (once through all the cards in the deck).

50 points minus—If you get rid of the pyramid during the first deal but still have cards in your hand or in the wastepile, score 50 points minus the number of cards in the wastepile.

35 points minus—If you get rid of the pyramid during the second deal, but still have cards in your hand or in the wastepile, score 35 points minus the number of cards in your hand and the wastepile.

20 points minus—If you get rid of the pyramid during the third deal, score 20 points minus the number of cards in your hand or the wastepile.

0 points minus—If you never do succeed in getting rid of your pyramid, deduct one point for each card left in the pyramid as well as each card left in your hand and the wastepile. That's right—a minus score!

"Par" is 0 for six matches. If you do better, you've won!

Quadrille

Other Names: Captive Queens, La Française, Partners

Space: Moderate

Level: Easy

Layout: The layout for this game is set up as you play. The design that is to be created appears on the opposite page.

Play: Start turning up cards from the deck. As soon as the fives and sixes appear, put them in place and start building on them.

On the fives you build down: **4 3 2 ace king.**
On the sixes you build up: **7 8 9 10 jack.**
The queens just sit in the middle and look regal.

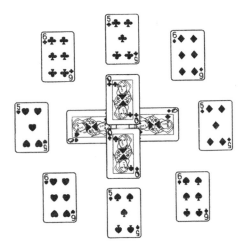

To win the game: Build the sixes up in suit to the jacks and the fives down in suit to the kings.

Redeals: Two.

Queen's Audience

Other Name: King's Audience

Space: Moderate

Level: Easy

Layout: Make a square of four cards to a side, as shown on the following page.

This is the queen's antechamber. The space inside it is the queen's audience. Into the audience will go the jacks, as they appear. They are the foundations.

To win the game: Build the foundations from jack to deuce in suit.

Special building rule: Before a jack can get into the queen's audience, an ace of the same suit has to go with him. That ace can come from the walls of the antechamber or from the stockpile. Put the ace under the jack.

Kings and queens get to come into the audience also, but only in pairs of the same suit. Put the king under the queen.

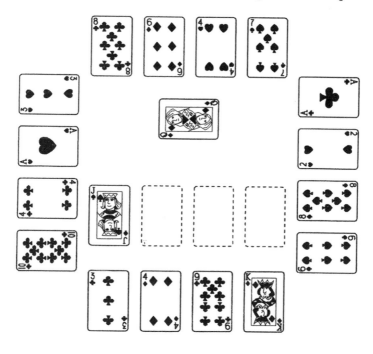

Play: Go through the cards one by one, building to the foundations and discarding queen and king sets into the audience.

Spaces in the antechamber wall should be filled right away from the top card of the wastepile or the stockpile.

Scorpion

Other Names: None
Space: Large
Level: Moderate
Layout: Deal a row of seven cards—four face down and three face up. Repeat this same pattern in a second and third row, overlapping the cards each time. Then deal out all the rest of the cards face up on top of this beginning setup. You'll have three cards left over at the end. Put them aside for a few minutes. Your layout will look like this:

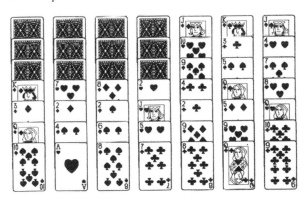

Play: Now you are going to build downward in suit on the exposed cards of the layout. But you are not limited to moving one card at a time. You may move any card that meets the requirements of rank and suit—even if it's covered with cards. You just move all the cards with it.

As columns are emptied, you can fill them with kings—along with the cards that are on top of them.

Nothing can be built on an ace.

When you have exhausted all chances for moves, take the three cards you set aside at the start and place one on each of the bottom cards of the left-hand columns. That picks up the game and can give you a few new moves.

To win the game: Build four kings, right on the layout, with their full suites, like this:

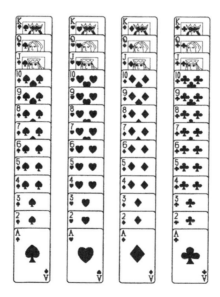

Crescent

Other Names: None
Space: Large
Level: Moderate
Decks: Two decks of cards
Layout: Select one ace and one king from each suit and place them in two rows, kings on top.

Then deal the rest of the cards in a semicircle around them in 16 piles. Put the first five cards face down, the top card face up.

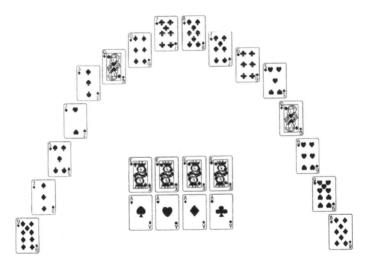

To win the game: Build aces up to kings in suit and kings down to aces in suit.
Play: Play whatever cards you can to the foundations. Then you can start building up or down on the layout in suit. When you move the top card of a pile, turn up the card underneath.

When you use up all the cards in a pile and you have an empty space, it cannot be refilled.

Shifting: When you can't make any more moves, take the bottom card from each pile and place it on top of the pile, face up. You need to do this with every pile before you stop to make any moves. You can make this unusual shifting move three times during the game; it's a little like having three redeals.

Reverse: When the top cards of two foundations of the same suit are in sequence, you can transfer one or more cards from one foundation to the other. The original ace and king may not be transferred.

Open Crescent

Play exactly the same as *Crescent*, but lay out the cards face up and spread them so that you can see them as you play.

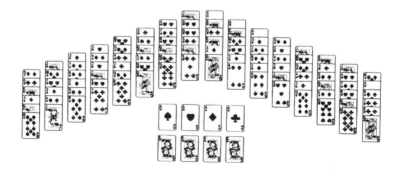

It's a more interesting game when strategy comes into play.

Diplomat

Other Names: None
Space: Moderate
Level: Easy
Decks: Two decks of cards

Similar to the one-pack *Streets and Alleys*, this game is fairly quick to set up and has lots of action.

Layout: Deal four columns of four overlapping cards, leaving space between them for two columns of side-by-side aces, which are the foundations as they become available.

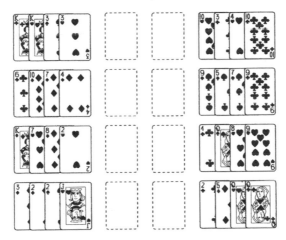

To win the game: Build the aces up in suit to kings.
Play: After making whatever moves you can to the foundations, you build downward on the exposed cards of the layout, regardless of suit.

When you can't make any more moves, start turning over the cards in your hand, one by one, playing what you can to the

layout. Place the unused cards in a wastepile. The top card of the wastepile, the card in your hand, and the exposed cards in the layout are all available to play onto foundations, onto the layout, and to fill any spaces that open up in the layout.
Redeals: One. Just turn over the wastepile.

Forty Thieves

Other Names: **Big Forty, Cadran, Napoleon at St. Helena, Roosevelt at San Juan**
Space: **Large**
Level: **Moderate**
Decks: **Two decks of cards**
Layout: Deal four rows of ten cards each, overlapping, as in the picture. Aces, as they become available, are moved up above the layout as foundations.

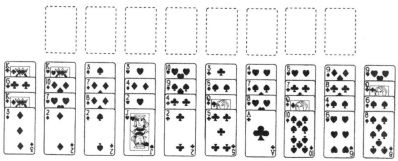

To win the game: Build all eight aces to kings in suit.
Play: First, build what you can to the foundations. Then build on the layout itself, downward in suit. For example, in the illustration above, the two of diamonds can be placed on the

three of diamonds. The ace of clubs can be played up to the foundation row. So can the 2. When you have exhausted all the possibilities, start going through the cards one by one, building onto foundations or layout or discarding the unplayable cards into a wastepile. The top card of that wastepile is available too.

When a space opens up in the layout, you can fill it with any card—one from the layout, the top card from the wastepile, or a card from your hand.

Grand Duchess

Other Names: Duchess of Luynes
Space: Small
Level: Moderate
Decks: Two decks of cards
Layout: Deal four cards in a row face up and an additional two cards face down to the side. Above them you'll be placing two rows of foundations, aces (one of each suit), and kings (one of each suit), as they become available.

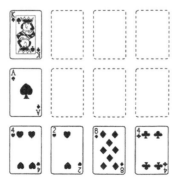

To win the game: Build the aces up in suit to kings and the kings down in suit to aces.

Play: Make any possible moves and then deal again—four cards on top of the cards you dealt before and two more cards face down to the side. Make your moves and continue in this fashion, until you've gone through the entire pack.

Then turn up the face-down cards, spreading them out and playing any cards you can to the foundations and making whatever moves are possible.

Redeals: Three (four times through the cards). When you're ready to redeal, pick up the piles in reverse order, so that the pile at the right is on the top. Put the face-down pile at the bottom.

The first two redeals are done just as before, spreading out the face-down pile at the end. The last one is different; don't deal any cards face down to the side. Just deal the four cards onto the layout. Don't build up a face-down pile at all.

Odd and Even

Other Names: None
Space: Moderate
Level: Moderate
Decks: Two decks of cards
Layout: Deal three rows of three cards each. These cards are available for building on the foundations.
Play: Start going through the cards in your hands one by one. As soon as the ace comes up, start a foundation row above the layout. As soon as a two comes up, place it in that row also, as shown in the picture.

Eventually, you need to place three more aces and three more deuces in the foundation row. One of each suit should be represented.

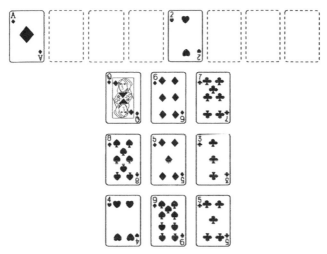

If you can't play the card from your hand onto the foundations, put it in a wastepile.

If a space opens up in the group of nine cards, fill it right away from the wastepile, or—if there is none—from your hand.

To win the game: Build the foundations upward in suit to full 13-card sequences—but you need to do it by twos!

The aces should build like this:

A 3 5 7 9 J K 2 4 6 8 10 Q

The deuces should build like this:

2 4 6 8 10 Q A 3 5 7 9 J K

Redeals: One.

Panama Canal

Other Names: Precedence, Panama Order of Precedence

Space: Moderate
Level: Easy
Decks: Two decks of cards

This is almost as simple as a game can get.

Layout: The layout starts with only one card in place—a king. That card will be followed by seven additional cards—the queen, jack, 10, 9, 8, 7, and six of any suit—as they become available. These are foundations.

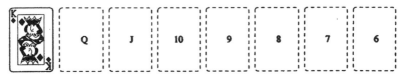

To win the game: You need to build each foundation downward and regardless of suit into a sequence of 13 cards.

Play: Start going through the pack, one card at a time. The catch is that you have to place the queen before you can put down the jack, and the jack must be in place before you can place the ten, and so on, down to the six. You are free, though, to build on the cards that are already in place. For example, you can put a queen on the king that is already on the table and a jack on the queen. Unplayable cards go into a wastepile whose top card is always available.

Circular sequence: Kings may be built on aces when the foundation card is something other than an ace or king.

Redeals: Two.

Pirate Gold

Other Names: None
Space: Moderate
Level: Easy
Decks: Two decks of cards
Layout: Deal ten cards face up on the table. You may place them in any convenient array, such as two rows of five cards each. If any two of these cards are a pair (two kings, two fives, etc.), cover each one with another face-up card from the deck. Continue in the same way, dealing cards so as to cover all the pairs you see.

To win the game: You must succeed in dealing out the whole deck.

The game comes out most of the time, but once in a while you will find yourself blocked with all ten cards in sight of different ranks. In fact, when *I* played the game as a boy, I turned it around: I considered that I won *only* if a block arose, so I did not *have* to deal out the whole deck to cover all the pairs.

Royal Cotillion

Other Names: None
Space: Large
Level: Moderate
Decks: Two decks of cards

There's something especially intriguing about this game, which is not surprising, considering that it is one of the most popular of the two-pack games.

Layout: First, to your left, deal out three rows of four cards each. To your right, deal out four rows of four cards each. Leave a space between them that is wide enough for two cards that will be the foundation columns. As they become available, move one ace and one deuce of each suit into this center section.

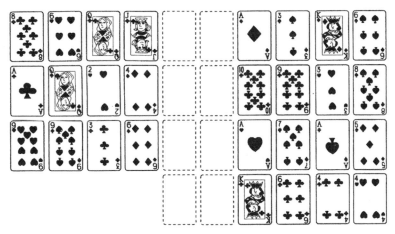

To win the game: Build the aces and deuces in the middle section upward by suit to a full 13-card sequence. The building must be by twos, as follows.

Aces should build:

A 3 5 7 9 J K 2 4 6 8 10 Q

Deuces should build:

2 4 6 8 10 Q A 3 5 7 9 J K

Play: Go through the cards one by one, building onto the foundations if you can or to the wastepile if you can't.

The cards that are off to your right can all be played onto the foundations, and as soon as spaces open up in this group, you can fill them from the wastepile— or if there is no wastepile, from your hand.

The cards that are off to the left, however, have only one active row—the bottom one. You can't move the cards in the second row until the bottom ones have been moved away. For example, in the illustration, only the nine of hearts, the nine of spades, the three of clubs, and the six of diamonds would be available to play onto the foundations. Spaces in the left-hand group are never filled in.

Spider

Other Names: None
Space: Large
Level: Difficult
Decks: Two decks of cards

This game has been called "the king of all solitaires."

Layout: Deal out 54 cards in ten piles as follows: six cards in the first four piles, five in the last six piles. Only the top cards should be face up. These piles are the foundations and the layout at the same time, and all the action takes place on them.

To win the game: Build eight sequences in downward order from kings to aces right on the layout. Once a sequence is built, it is discarded. So to win the game is to have nothing on the table.

Play: After you lay out the cards, make all the moves you can, building down, regardless of suit. Note, however, that even though you're permitted to build regardless of suit, you limit yourself when you do it. You are permitted to move a group of cards as a unit only when they are in suit and in correct rank— so while you would never be able to win the game by making only moves that were in suit, it is certainly better to build in suit, if you have the choice.

When you move an entire pile, leaving a blank space, you may move any available card or group of cards into it. Keep in mind, though, that a king cannot move, except into a blank space. It cannot be placed on an ace.

When you can't make any more moves, deal ten more cards, one on each pile. And again, make whatever moves you can. Follow this procedure for the entire game, dealing another ten cards whenever you're stuck.

All spaces must be filled before you are allowed to deal another ten cards onto the layout.

After you have put together a complete sequence, you don't have to discard it right away. You may be able to use it to help build other sequences.

The Sultan of Turkey

**Other Names: The Sultan, The Harem, Emperor
            of Germany**
Space: Moderate
Level: Easy
Decks: Two decks of cards
Layout: Remove the eight kings and one ace of hearts from the pack and place them as shown in the illustration. Add four cards from the pack on both sides of the kings. You can use these cards to build onto the foundations.

All the kings—and the ace—are foundations, except for the king of hearts that is in the middle of the square. Don't build on it.

To win the game: Build all the kings (except the middle king of hearts) up to queens, in suit—and build the ace of hearts to a queen, also.

Of course, in order to build up the kings, you're going to need to add an ace before starting on the deuces.

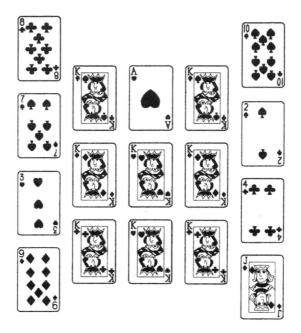

Play: Go through the cards one by one and start adding to the foundations. Any cards you can't use go into a wastepile.

As soon as a space opens up in the layout, fill it at once, either from the wastepile or from your hand.

Redeals: Two. Shuffle well before going through the cards a second and third time.

The most delightful aspect of this game is the way it looks when you win. Try it.

ALL-FOURS GAMES

Card players have enjoyed games of the All-Fours group, including *Seven-Up* and its many variations, since the late 1600s. Having its origins in England, *Seven-Up,* along with *Whist* and *Put,* was popular in the early 1700s and for years competed with Poker as the favorite gambling game in the United States.

Seven-Up

Players and Deck Used: The game requires two, three, or four persons (when they are playing as partners, two against two) and a full deck of 52 cards. The cards rank as follows: ace (high), king, queen, jack, 10...2 (low).

Beginning the Game: The players cut for high card to determine the first deal and partners (when four play). Highest cut becomes the dealer, and high cuts play as partners against low cuts. After the shuffle and cut, the dealer gives six cards to each player, three at a time, in rotation from left to right. After completing the deal, the dealer faces, or turns up, the next card to show the "trump" suit, any card of which will win over any card of another suit. If the card turned up is a jack, the dealer scores 1 point. If more than two persons are playing, only the dealer and first player can look at their hands until the turned-up card is accepted or rejected as trump. The deal passes to the left at the end of each hand.

Ranking of Cards in *Seven-Up*

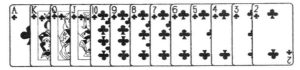

The Goals: The goals of the game are: (a) to hold the highest and lowest trumps in play; (b) to turn the jack for trumps or to capture it in play, and (c) to capture cards in play that count toward game.

Making the Trump: The player seated to the dealer's left has the first right to *stand* or *beg*. If she is satisfied with the trump turned, she "stands" and leads (plays the first card) to the first *trick* (sequence of cards played). If she begs, the dealer must either say "Take it" and give her a 1-point *gift* to let the trump stand, or deal three new cards to each player and turn up a new trump. The dealer, however, cannot give her the 1-point gift if it will give her *game* (winning) point. If the dealer chooses to give each player three more cards and turns up a trump that is the same as the first one, the dealer then repeats the process until she turns up a card of a different suit. This process is called *running the deck*. If she turns up the jack of the rejected trump suit while running the deck, she does not score 1 point for doing so. If a new trump is turned up while running the deck, all players keep their best six cards, discarding the others. However, if the dealer runs the whole deck without turning up a different trump, she collects the cards and redeals.

The player seated to the dealer's left leads any card. If the card is a trump, the players must follow suit, if possible. If the card is not a trump, the players must follow suit, but, if unable to do so, they may either play a trump or discard. The highest card in the suit led wins, unless the trick is "trumped," in which case the highest trump wins. The winner of each trick leads to the next trick.

Scoring: The players score points as follows:

> *High*—the highest trump in play. Player to whom dealt gets 1 point.
>
> *Low*—the lowest trump in play. Player to whom dealt gets 1 point.
>
> *Jack*—jack of trumps. If in play, scored by the dealer turning it up as trump or by the player taking it in a trick: 1 point.
>
> *Game*—won by person holding cards with the highest point count taken during play: 1 point.

In counting points for game, ten counts as 10 points; aces, 4; kings, 3; queens, 2; jacks, 1. If there is a tie for "game" between the dealer and a nondealer, the latter wins; otherwise, no one scores game point. If a player holds the only trump in play, she will win high and low, and, if the card she holds is the trump jack, she will win high, low, and jack.

Game: The player taking the greatest number of points in one hand wins the game. Many Seven-Up enthusiasts, however, prefer playing successive hands, usually two to three, until one of the players scores 7 or 10 points, as agreed to at the beginning of the game. In the latter procedure, the first player to score 7 (or 10) points wins the game. For example, if the dealer needs 1 point to "go out" and she turns the jack of trumps, she wins. If both players take enough points to win the game in the same hand, they score their points in this order: high, low, jack, and game.

Remedies and Penalties: If a player intentionally or unintentionally exposes a card, she places it face up on the table and plays it when it is legal to do so. If all players agree, they may allow the offender to keep the card in her hand during the play.

A player who *revokes,* or fails to follow suit when she could have done so, incurs penalties if she does not correct the revoke before the trick is *quitted* (placed face down) and the next lead made. If she does not correct the revoke, she cannot "go out" in that hand, nor can she cumulatively score more than 6 points. Additionally, if the trump jack is not in play, she forfeits 1 point of her score; if the trump jack is in play, she forfeits 2 points.

Many players prefer a stiffer penalty for a revoke, such as forfeiture of the game.

Variation: If a player begs in a three-hand game and the dealer decides to give her 1 point instead of running the deck, she must also give 1 point to the other nondealer. If the first player in a three-hand game stands, the next player has the right to stand or beg. If both stand, the first player leads to the first trick.

POKER GAMES

Poker evolved slowly from an old French game called *Gilet*, which in turn probably had its origins in the Italian game of *Primero*. During the reign of Charles IX (1560–1574), notable for its bloody civil wars between the Catholics and Huguenot Protestants, *Gilet* became the game of *Brelan*. By the time of the French Revolution, the game of *Brelan* developed into *Bouillotte*, which included such devices as the blind, freeze-out, raise, bluff, and table stakes—all of which are common to modern-day Poker.

Bouillotte also gave rise to *Ambigu*, which supplied the draw, and the English game of *Brag*, which was largely a bluffer's game. These three games—*Bouillotte*, *Ambigu*, and *Brag*—shaped modern-day Poker, along with the adoption of the 52-card deck by 1835 and the introduction of five, instead of three, dealt cards.

Basic Poker

Two to eight persons play Poker with a 52-card deck. The players sometimes limit the number of people allowed to participate according to the game being played and the number of cards needed to fill out the hands. A joker may be added to the deck by mutual consent, and, if the joker is added, it is wild and is used as the holder wishes. The cards rank: ace (high)...2 (low). But sometimes at the beginning of a game, the players agree to an ace's being used as high *or* low, such as in low sequences, or runs.

Seating: Players usually sit where they please, but some prefer to determine the seating arrangement by dealing each person one card face up, letting the person with low sit to the dealer's left, next low to his left, and so forth. Ties are broken by cutting for low card. The players may decide where a newcomer sits by mutual agreement, by the method above, or by some other means of choice.

Chips: By mutual consent, one player assumes the role of banker and takes charge of exchanging chips for money and for settling accounts at the end of the card session. (Matchsticks, beans, etc., may be substituted for chips.) Again by mutual consent, the players decide on the value of white, red, blue, and yellow chips.

Before the Game Begins: Poker players should decide the following at the start of the game: (a) amount of the ante (preliminary bet made before the deal), as well as who antes (sometimes the dealer only, but usually all players); (b) a bet/raise limit; (c) a time set to stop the card session. Instead of setting a time to end a session, some players prefer *freeze-out*. In freeze-out, all players begin the card session with the same number of chips, and as soon as any player loses his chips, he retires from the session, which continues until one player has won all the chips. Sometimes the players also set a limit to the number of times that a bet may be raised, which oftentimes is three raises, or *bumps*.

Beginning the Game: Players customarily determine the first dealer by having the cards dealt around face up, one at a time, until a jack falls—the person who receives the first jack deals. (Some players prefer to draw or cut for high or low card to determine the first dealer.) But before the cards are actually dealt, the dealer and, sometimes, the other players, depending on the game being played, ante chips on the middle of the table to begin the "pot."

The shuffle and cut are as in other card games. However, the person sitting to the dealer's right may decline to cut the deck. If he does decline, the players to his right, in turn, may cut or decline to do so. If all players decline, the deal proceeds. The dealer gives each player his cards, one at a time, in clockwise rotation, beginning with the person to his left. (This applies to all poker games.) The dealer cannot deal the last card; instead, he shuffles this card with the discards to rebuild his dealing stock.

The Stripped Deck: If there are only three or four people playing, they may choose to strip the deck of its twos, threes, and, sometimes, fours. If the players strip the deck and aces are low, an 8-high straight would consist of 8, 7, 6, 5, and ace.

The Goal: The goal of each round of poker is to hold or draw to the best hand, thereby winning the pot or a portion of it, depending on the game being played. In determining the winner(s) of each pot, the custom among poker players is to "let the cards speak for themselves."

Poker hands rank from high to low, as follows:

1. Five of a kind. Five cards of the same rank, or denomination, which is possible only when the joker is included in the deck and/or other wild cards are named.

2. **Royal straight flush.** An ace, king, queen, jack, and 10 sequence, or run, in any suit.

3. **Straight flush.** A five-card sequence, or run, in a suit ranked by its highest card. For example, a player would call his club sequence of 10, 9, 8, 7, and 6 a straight flush, 10 high. A 10-high straight flush would rank over a 9-high straight flush.

4. **Four of a kind,** which is ranked by its denomination. For example, four queens rank over four jacks.

5. **Full house.** A combination of three cards of one denomination and two cards of another: for example, three kings and two tens. The "triplet" (three of a kind) decides rank. For example, three kings and two tens rank over three queens and two jacks (or three kings rank over three queens).

6. **Flush.** Any five cards in a suit, but not in sequence. A player ranks a flush by the highest card in the flush.

7. **Straight.** A sequence, or run, of five cards in various suits, which is ranked by its highest card.

8. **Three of a kind,** or three cards of the same denomination, which are ranked by their denomination.

9. **Two pairs of any denominations,** which are ranked by the highest pair. For example, jacks and fives would rank over tens and eights.

10. **One pair of any denomination** with three unmatched cards. A pair is ranked by denomination.

11. **High card.** A hand with none of the combinations listed above, ranked by its highest card. In case of a tie, the player holding a card of the next-higher denomination wins.

Ties: If the high cards in flushes tie, the next higher cards determine the winner. Ties in straight flushes, full houses, flushes, and straights divide the pot. In dividing such pots, the players usually cut for high card to determine the ownership of odd chips. If players hold four of a kind, a full house (in a seven-card game), two pairs, or one pair tie, their unmatched cards break the tie by rank. If high cards tie, the other cards again break the tie by rank. **Note:** In cases where one of two tying hands has a joker, many players hold that the natural hand, the one without the joker, wins. Other players hold the opposite view, because the odds of drawing a joker are less than drawing a natural hand. But the latter group also holds that if both tying hands have multiple wild cards, the one with the fewer wild cards wins. If a poker group wants to break ties involving wild cards by one of the methods just discussed, they should mutually agree to the method at the start of the game to avoid disputes and, perhaps, hard feelings. Otherwise, tied hands split the pot according to guidelines set forth in the paragraph above.

Table Stakes: While a hand is in progress, a player may, with the consent of the other players, raise the betting limit to *table stakes*, which is the amount of chips he has on the table at the time. No one can raise the amount of the table stakes after looking at any of his cards. If another player does not have enough chips to *call*, or *see*, the table stakes raise, he may call a *sight* of the last bettor's cards for what chips he does have and separate that part of the pot from the rest.

The other players continue their calls and raises; some of these players also may call for a sight and thus fragment the pot further. If the person calling for a sight holds the winning hand during the showdown, he wins only that part of the pot for which he called his sight; the other players decide on the winner of the rest of the pot on the merits of their respective hands.

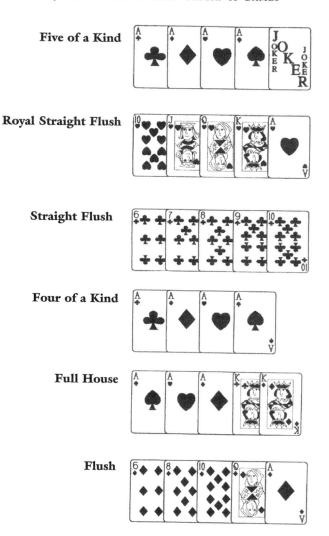

Five of a Kind

Royal Straight Flush

Straight Flush

Four of a Kind

Full House

Flush

An accelerated variation of table stakes is the *double-up game*, wherein each player to the left of the dealer may in turn call for

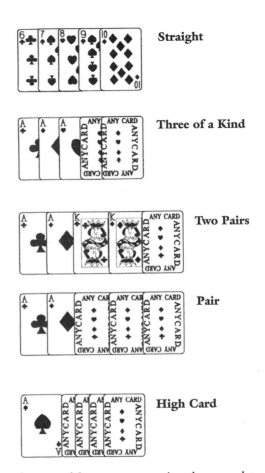

table stakes raises that would stop at a previously agreed-to number of such raises—usually up to six.

Remedies and Penalties: In case of a misdeal, the dealer deals again with the same pack. If a card is exposed in cutting or in reuniting a pack, the dealer must shuffle the deck again and redeal. Other misdeals include: an uncut or improperly reunited deck; a card placed face up in the deck; an incomplete or otherwise imperfect deck. If an extra but unexposed card is accidentally given to a player, the dealer can restore it to the top of the deck or continue his deal with it, whichever action is more appropriate.

If a player has a hand of fewer or more than the cards needed for the game, if he has looked at them, and if he has bet on them, his hand is foul. He then must, upon discovery, abandon the hand, forfeiting the chips he has put into the pot and even the pot itself if he won it on that deal. If a player finds that he has too many or too few cards and he has not looked at them, he may request that the dealer remedy the card count by drawing cards from his hand or by dealing additional cards to his hand to leave it at the correct number of cards. However, if more than one hand is irregular in the deal and cannot be easily remedied, the cards must be shuffled, cut, and dealt again.

If a player has looked at any of his cards, he cannot ask for a new deal unless the deck is found to be imperfect. A deal out of turn or with the wrong deck must be stopped before it is completed; otherwise, it stands.

If a player bets, calls, and/or raises out of sequence, the turn returns to the appropriate player. However, any chips the offender put in the pot remain there, and when his turn comes around, his bet, call, or raise is regarded as already made. In effect, he can make no further bets or raises until his turn comes around again, if it does. If he owes chips in addition to those put in the pot earlier, he makes up the difference. If he put too many chips in the pot, he forfeits them to the pot.

If a player announces a bet, call, or raise out of turn but does not put the chips in the pot, his announcement is void and the turn to bet, call, or raise reverts to the appropriate player.

If any player puts more chips in the pot than are required by a bet, call, or raise, he forfeits the excess chips to the pot. If he puts too few chips in the pot, he must make up the difference.

Straight, or Bluff, Poker

Straight Poker, the immediate forerunner of all modern-day poker games, at first required four players and a 20-card deck (aces, kings, queens, jacks, and tens), with each person being dealt a five-card hand. Although the original game is still a popular two-hand game, it is now more often played by two to eight persons with a 52-card deck.

In *Straight Poker*, only the dealer antes. After she has done so and the cards are shuffled and cut, she gives each player five cards face down, one at a time, and in clockwise rotation. Beginning with the player at the dealer's left, each person, in turn, may drop from the game, check (put the lowest value of chips in the pot to remain in the game), or make a bet, placing her chips in the middle of the table. Once a bet is made, the other players remaining in the game must either call the bet or drop out of the game. A player calling a bet may also raise it, which requires the other players to call the raise if they want to stay in the game. During this round of betting and raising, a player holding a weak hand might try to bluff the others out of the game by betting and/or raising excessively, hoping thereby to "buy" the pot. If no one sees the bet (meets or equals it), the bettor wins the pot without having to show her cards. If the bet or bet and raises are called, all players still in the game expose their hands face up for the showdown. The best poker hand wins the pot.

Draw Poker

In *Draw Poker* each player antes, and the dealer gives each person five cards face down, one at a time, and in clockwise rotation. After receiving and examining his cards, each player, beginning with the one at the dealer's left, drops from the game, bets, or checks the bet of the person at his left. After all players pass or after all bets and raises have been called, each player discards his unwanted cards face down, and the dealer gives him replacements.

After the players examine the cards they received on the draw, a second round of betting takes place. Following this second betting interval, the players lay their cards face up on the table for the showdown. The person holding the best hand wins.

Variations: In the game described above, a player may open the betting without holding a pair. However, many players prefer playing a variation of *Draw Poker* called *Jacks or Better*, or *Jackpots*. In this variation, a player must hold a pair of jacks or a hand better than jacks in order to open the betting. In this variation, if no one can open the betting, everyone antes another chip to the pot and the cards are gathered up, shuffled, cut, and dealt again. If a person opens the betting and is later discovered not to have held the requisite cards to open, he must pay a penalty, which usually is double the size of the final pot.

Another variation of *Draw Poker* is *Progressive Draw Poker*, wherein a player needs jacks or better to open the betting. If no one can open with jacks or better, everyone antes another chip to the pot while the cards are gathered up, shuffled, cut, and dealt again. On the second deal, a player must have queens or better to open the betting—hence the title *Progressive Draw Poker*. If no one can open with queens or better, the third deal requires kings or better; the fourth deal requires aces or better; the fifth deal returns to jacks or better; and so forth. Players like this variation because it builds large pots quickly.

Another popular variation is *Pass and Out*. In this variation, a player may open the betting holding nothing more than a pair, but in each turn he must either bet or drop out. He cannot "pass," or check, the betting to the next player.

Draw Poker with a Joker

While playing Draw Poker, as well as some other games, some players like to include the joker, or *bug*, in the deck. The joker affects the game as follow:

1. The person holding the joker may use it as any card she wishes with one exception: She cannot use the joker in a flush to replace a card she already holds. For example, she cannot use it as an ace with an ace-high flush and call that flush a double-ace high flush or straight flush. Nonetheless, the joker makes it possible for a player to hold as many as five of a kind, which ranks over all other hands.

2. For showdown purposes, if two hands are equal in all respects, the tied hands split the pot, unless the players agree at the start of the game that a natural hand ranks over one with a joker or other wild cards.

Lowball

Lowball is a variation of *Draw Poker,* in which the lowest-ranking hand, rather than the highest-ranking, wins the pot. There are no minimum requirements to open the pot, and straights and flushes do not count. In *Lowball,* aces are always low; hence, a pair of aces ranks lower than a pair of deuces, and the lowest hand possible is a 5, 4, 3, 2, and ace, whether it is made up of one or two suits.

During play, a player may check, or pass. If no one bets and the dealer has called for bets twice, a showdown takes place and the lowest hand wins the ante.

Ranking of cards in *Lowball*

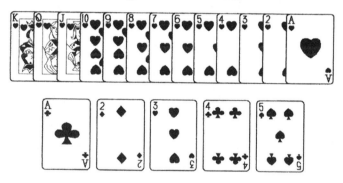

Lowest hand of any suit or combination of suits

Deuces Wild

Deuces (twos) *Wild* is another variation of *Draw Poker with a Joker.* Deuces affect the game as follows:

1. Each deuce, or two, ranks as a joker and may be used as any

card its holder wishes, except the duplicate of a card he already holds in a flush, as explained in *Draw Poker with a Joker*. The players also may wish to include the joker in a *Deuces Wild* game.

2. For showdown purposes, tied hands split the pot, unless the players agree at the start of the game that the hand with no or the fewest wild cards breaks such ties.

Wild Widow

Wild Widow is a variation of *Draw Poker*. The two games differ as follows:

1. The dealer gives the players four cards one at a time face down, turns the next card face up as the Wild Widow in the middle of the table, and then deals one more card face down to each person.

2. If a player holds a card or cards that match the face-up Wild Widow (the designated wild card), she may call and use them in any way she chooses, as in *Deuces Wild*. The players also may include the joker in the deck.

Spit in the Ocean

Spit in the Ocean is another variation of *Draw Poker*. The two games differ as follows:

1. The dealer gives each player four cards face down and then turns the next card, which is wild, face up in the middle of the table.

2. If a player holds a card or cards that match the face-up card, he may call and use them in any way he chooses, as in *Deuces Wild*.

3. Each player regards the face-up card as the fifth card of his hand, and he bases his draw on four cards only.

Five-Card Stud

Typically, there is no ante in a stud game, unless one has been agreed to by the players; however, if one player antes, all ante. After the shuffle and cut, the dealer gives each person one card face down (the hole card) and then one card face up, in clockwise rotation. In *Five-and Seven-Card Stud,* the dealer customarily announces the first bettor in each betting interval by pointing out the high card or best face-up hand. The dealer likewise points out possible hands, such as possible straights, flushes, and so forth.

The players examine their face-down cards, and the person receiving the highest face-up card must open the betting or drop from the game. In case of a tie for high card, the person receiving the first high card bets. If this person drops from the game, the person with the next-highest card bets, and a betting interval follows.

After the first round of betting is completed, the dealer then gives each player still in the game a second face-up card. With two cards placed face up, the highest exposed poker combination bets first or drops from the game, as above. Thus, an ace, king outranks a queen, jack, and a pair outranks high cards. After the second round of betting, the dealer gives each active player a third face-up card, which is followed by the person with the best exposed hand opening the betting interval. Finally, the dealer gives each active player a fourth face-up card, for a total of five cards, and again the player with the best exposed hand initiates the betting interval, which is followed by the showdown. The player with the best hand wins the pot.

Remedies and Penalties: If the dealer accidentally exposes a card before a betting interval is completed, she buries the card and gives the top card to the player who would have received it if the other card had not been exposed. She completes that round of dealing with the person whose card was accidentally exposed and buried.

Mexican Stud

Mexican Stud is a variation of *Five-Card Stud*. The two games differ as follows:

1. The dealer deals all five cards face down.

2. On receiving her second, third, fourth, and fifth cards, each player may decide which of her face-down cards to turn face up. Each player must turn a card face up before each round of betting.

Seven-Card Stud

As in *Five-Card Stud,* the ante is optional. The dealer begins the game by giving the players two cards face down and a third card face up, one at a time, which is followed by a betting interval as described in *Five-Card Stud* above. The dealer then gives each player her fourth, fifth, and sixth cards face up in three rounds of dealing. After each such round of the deal, the players hold a betting interval. Finally, the dealer gives each person her seventh, and last, card face down, which is followed by a final round of betting and the showdown.

In the showdown, each player selects her best five cards as her poker hand. Only in the case of tied hands would the players use their other two cards; in this event, the higher card(s) would break the tie.

Other than the number of cards and betting intervals, *Five-* and *Seven-Card Stud* are the same game.

Baseball

Baseball is the same game as *Five-*and *Seven-Card Stud*, with the following exceptions:

1. All nines, whether face up or down, and threes face down ("in the hole") are wild.

2. If a player receives a face-up three, he must either "buy the pot" (double its value) or drop out of the game. If he buys the pot, thus staying in the game, all threes are wild whether face up or down (in the hole.)

3. If a player receives a face-up four, he receives another face-up card immediately as a bonus card. A four dealt face down (in the hole) does not earn a bonus card.

As in other Stud games, the player chooses his best five cards as his poker hand in the showdown.

High-Low Poker

The concept of *High-Low* can be applied to most poker games. When *High-Low* is applied, the holder of the high hand always wins the odd chip.

The lowest-making hand is called "the run hand," and it consists of a hand of different suits whose value is less than a pair. Thus, the lowest run possible is a 2, 3, 4, 5, and 7 of mixed suits. The highest card determines the rank of a runt.

SHOWDOWN GAMES

Black Jack (Twenty-One)

Number of Players and Deck Used: Any number of persons may play this game (four to eight being best) with a 52-card deck and chips. The cards rank as follows: Each ace counts as either 1 or 11, depending only on the player's need; each king, queen, jack, or ten counts as 10; each nine...two counts as its pip, or index, value. (*Pips* are the markings on the cards that indicate the numerical value of the card. A ten, which has 10 pips, has a numerical value of 10.)

Chips and Bet: Before the game actually gets under way, the players agree what number of chips constitutes a minimum and maximum wager, or bet. Each player, except the dealer, must place her bet on the table in front of herself before she receives any cards at the beginning of each round of play. The dealer does not need to make a bet, because she is playing against each of the other players for whatever their individual bets may be.

Beginning the Game: In home games, the players draw or cut cards for first deal. High cut wins. The dealer shuffles, and any player may cut. The dealer then *burns a card*, that is, she turns a card from the top of the deck, makes it visible to all players, and turns it face up on the bottom of the deck, if it is not an ace. If the card is an ace, the shuffle, cut, and burn procedure is repeated. Some players will allow the dealer to slip the ace into the deck and to face and burn another card without repeating the entire shuffle, cut, and burn procedure. Then, in rotation from left to right, the dealer gives each player, including herself, one card face down, and then she deals each player, except herself, a second card face down. She deals her second card face up.

The Goal: The goal of the game is the same for all players: to hold cards whose combined pip value is 21, or the nearest possible number below 21 without exceeding 21.

"Taking Hits" and Settling Wagers: If the dealer has dealt herself an ace and any other card with a pip value of 10, she announces "Black Jack" or "Twenty-One" and collects the wagers of the other players. By agreement before the game starts, the dealer may collect double the original bet. If the dealer does not announce Black Jack, each player looks at her face-down cards and mentally calculates their pip value. If any player holds a Black Jack, she announces it and collects double her bet from the dealer.

After the Black Jacks, if any, have been announced and settlements made, each player in turn, beginning with the one at the dealer's left, looks at the dealer's face-up card to help her decide whether or not she will *stand pat* or *take a hit* and thereby run the risk of going *bust*, or having cards whose count exceeds 21 points. If she is satisfied with her cards, she will say, "I'll stand pat," thereby letting the dealer know that she does not want any more cards. If she is not satisfied with her cards, she will say, "Hit me," thereby letting the dealer know that she wants one more card. If she wants more than one hit, she will say, "Hit me again" for each additional card she wants until she is satisfied or goes bust.

Most players will ask for a hit if the pip value of their cards is 16 or less. If the pip value of their cards is 17, most players will stand pat, unless they have cause to believe that the dealer's cards have a larger combined pip value. One such cause might be that the dealer's face-up card is an 8, 9, 10, or ace. At this point, most players assess the dealer's demeanor and follow their intuition.

If the player asks for a hit and the total pip value of her cards exceeds 21, she admits that fact and forfeits her bet to the dealer. However, if the total pip value of her cards does not exceed 21 and she does not want to chance another hit, she will stand pat. Thus, each player in rotation will decide to stand pat or take a hit.

When the time comes for the dealer to make a decision to stand pat or take a hit, she turns up her hole, or face-down, card to view. The face-up cards of her opponents and her intuition will prompt her to stand pat or take a hit. Most dealers will stand pat on 17, unless their intuition prompts otherwise. (Some players make it a rule that the dealer must stand pat on 17 and collect or pay accordingly.) If the dealer overdraws or exceeds 21, she pays all players their wagers if the pip value of their cards is greater than the pip value of her cards. She does not pay players holding cards with the same or a lower pip value than the cards she holds. (All ties are won by the dealer.)

In addition to the procedures above for standing pat, taking hits, and settling bets, the following variation of play may occur: If the dealer deals a player two aces or another pair whose pip value is 10 each, the player may *split the pair*, advance a second bet equal to the first, and play the aces or other pair as two separate hands. The dealer then deals a card face down to each card of the pair. When a player splits a pair, she must stand pat, take a hit, or otherwise play out the first hand of the pair before playing the second hand.

After the first round of play is completed, the dealer deals the next round from the unused stock. When the entire stock is exhausted, the dealer gathers all discards and repeats the shuffle, cut, and burn procedure given above. The deal customarily passes to a player who has Black Jack when the dealer has not done so at the same time. When this happens, the dealer completes the play for that hand before passing the deck and deal to the new dealer.

Remedies: If it is discovered that the dealer failed to burn a card, she must on demand shuffle the remainder of the deck and do so. A misdealt card can be accepted or rejected by its recipient.

Variations: While the version of Black Jack above is probably the one played most often, there are other versions with slight variations. One such variation is that the dealer gives each player, including herself, one card face down and the second card face up.

A good rule to follow is to make sure that all players understand which version and variations will be in force before starting a game. This is especially important if you are playing in professional gambling casinos like those found in states with legalized gambling.

Spanish Monte

Spanish Monte, a Latin American gambling game, requires a deck of 40 cards (a 52-card deck stripped of its eights, nines, and tens). Any number of players may participate.

Beginning the Game: The players draw or cut for low card to determine the first dealer-banker. Ace is lowest. After the shuffle and cut, the dealer, holding the deck face down, draws two cards from the bottom of the deck and turns them face up on the table as the bottom layout. Next, he draws two cards from the top of the deck and turns them face up on the table as the top layout. After the dealer forms these two layouts, each player places his bet(s) on one or both layouts.

The Play and Settling Up: After all bets are made, the dealer turns the deck face up to expose the bottom card, which is the port, or gate, card. If the suit of the port card matches the suit of either card in the top layout, the dealer pays all bets on that layout. The same holds true if the suit of the port card matches the suit of either card in the bottom layout. If the suit of the port card does not match the suits in either the top or bottom layout, the dealer collects all bets made. Thus, the dealer pays for matches in either or both layouts and collects for no matches.

After the dealer and players settle all bets, the former turns the deck face down and gathers up and discards the four layout cards along with the port card. The dealer then forms two new layouts, as above, and again turns the deck face up to expose a new port card. Thus, the game proceeds until the deck is exhausted.

EUCHRE GAMES

The euchre group of card games has been closely associated with four different countries. In the United States, the game played is *Euchre;* in Ireland, *Spoil Five;* in England, *Napoleon;* and in France, *Écarté.* Enthusiasts in each country developed their own variations of the game.

The old Spanish game of *Triumphe,* mentioned in an early sixteenth-century manuscript, probably provided the origin of euchre. The French modified *Triumphe* and renamed it *French Ruff.* With the passage of time and more modification, this game became *Écarté,* which was introduced by the French into the United States in Louisiana.

An interesting observation about these games is that the king outranks the ace in both *Écarté* and some versions of *Rams (Ramsch),* a German descendant of euchre. In the older games, the king always headed each suit, and the ace was the lowest card. It was only after political upheaval that the ace became the highest-ranking card.

Another theory of euchre's origin is that the game might have resulted from an effort to play the Irish game of *Spoil Five* with a *Piquet* deck. The word *euchre* is of unknown origin, and it means, as does the word *spoil* in *Spoil Five,* to stop or trick the maker of the trump from taking three tricks. An interesting note about this theory is that *Spoil Five* inherited its highest trump card, the trump five, from the Irish game of *Five Fingers*, which, in turn, has its origins in an even older Irish card game called *Maw*, which was popular during the early seventeenth century. Since the *Piquet* deck had no five, it is believed that the players used the second-ranking trump, the jack, to head the trump suit, which is, of course, characteristic of euchre.

Euchre

Euchre is a game for four persons (two against two as partners), three persons, or two persons, the last two being played as cutthroat. The game requires a deck of 32 cards (ace, king, queen, jack, 10, 9, 8, 7), or 28 cards (ace through 8), or 24 cards (ace through 9). The joker is sometimes optionally used.

Cards rank as follows: *in trump suit*—the right bower (jack of trumps), the left bower (jack of same color), and then trump ace, king, queen, 10, 9, 8, and 7; *in suit of same color*—ace, king, queen, 10, 9, 8, 7; *in suits of opposite color*—ace, king, queen, jack, 10, 9, 8, and 7. If the joker is used, it is the highest-ranking trump, outranking both bowers.

Beginning the Game: In the draw for deal, with ace being low, low draws play as partners against the high draws. If the joker is drawn, the player must draw again. After the shuffle and cut, the dealer gives each player five cards (either three and two or two and three), in rotation to the left. The dealer turns the next card face up to propose the trump suit. After each hand, the deal passes to the left.

The dealer must redeal if the deck is imperfect, if there is a card face up in the deck, if she gives the wrong number of cards to any player, if she turns more than one card for trump, or if she does not deal the same number of cards to each player in the same round.

Rank of cards in play in *Euchre*

If hearts are trump

If hearts are trump, suits of same color

If hearts are trump, suits of opposite color

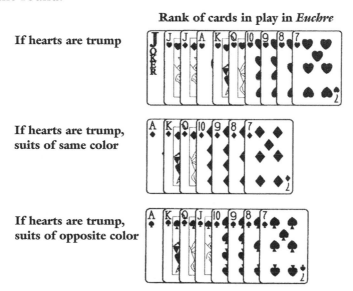

If the joker is turned for trump, the dealer may, before looking at her hand, declare the suit that the joker represents to be trump. The players, however, may select such a suit for trump before the game or hand gets under way.

Making the Trump: The player to the dealer's left may say, "I order it up," meaning that she accepts the card turned and thus proposed as trump by the dealer, or she may pass. If the trump is ordered up, the dealer must immediately discard a card face down from her hand, though she does not take the trump card into her hand before it is her turn to play to the first trick.

If the player to the left of the dealer passes, the dealer's partner may order up the trump by saying, "I assist," or she may pass. If she passes, the next player in rotation has the same option. If all three pass, the dealer may take up the trump or pass. If the dealer passes, she puts face down the card turned as trump. If all four pass, each player in rotation to the left has one chance to name a suit trump, but not the one just rejected, or again pass. The first suit named becomes trump. If all four players pass a second time, the deal is void and passes to the left.

After the trump is taken up, any player may ask the trump maker to name the trump suit, but no one can demand to know its denomination. If the trump is the same color as the face-down proposed trump, this is called *making it next*; if it is the other color, it is called *crossing the suit*.

The person who orders up, takes up, or names the trump may play alone against both opponents. In this case, her partner lays her cards face down on the table and takes no part in the play, but she does share in her partner's victory or defeat. One partner cannot object to the other's going it alone, but the latter must announce her decision to do so when she declares the trump suit. Formerly, a dealer whose partner had assisted was allowed to go it alone; this practice is still observed in some localities.

The Goal: The goal of the trump maker and her partner is to take at least three of a possible five tricks. The goal of the opponents is to *euchre*, or stop, the trump maker from taking three tricks.

The Play: The person to the dealer's left or to the left of the player "going it alone," whatever the case might be, leads any card, and each player in succession plays a card in the same suit, if possible. If not possible, she must either play a trump or discard. It is not necessary to take the trick. If the trick is trumped, the highest trump wins. The winner of each trick leads to the next trick. The winner of each trick must gather it up and quit it, that is, turn it face down. Once quitted, no player may examine the trick until the end of the hand. After five tricks have been quitted and tallied for score, the deal passes to the left.

Scoring: If the trump maker and her partner take three tricks, they win the hand and the game. If they do not take three tricks, they are euchred and they lose the game.

Many euchre enthusiasts prefer playing a longer game to a score of 5, 7, or 10 points, as agreed to at the beginning of the session. In these games, if the trump maker and her partner take three or four out of five tricks, they score 1 point toward game. If they win all five tricks for a *march*, they score 2 points. If the trump maker "goes it alone," she gets 4 points for a march. If the trump maker and her partner fail to get three tricks, they are euchred and their opponents score 2 points. Euchre players can use a long-game-scoring procedure with the one-hand, ten-minute game for wagering purposes. In the latter procedure, a scorekeeper keeps a cumulative score until the game ends.

Remedies and Penalties: If a person mistakenly "orders up" or "assists," her side must accept the burden of declaration. If a player names for trump the suit of the rejected proposed trump, her side may not make the trump for that deal.

If a player leads out of turn and everyone plays to the lead, that lead is regarded as valid, and the game continues. However, if the mistake is caught before everyone plays to the erroneous lead, any player may demand that the lead be retracted, left face up on the table, and played at the first legal opportunity. The persons who played to the erroneous lead may restore their cards to their hands without penalty. The opponent who will play last in the next lead of the offending side has the right to name the suit to be led.

If a revoke is made but caught before the trick is quitted, the player may substitute a card. However, if the revoke is not caught until after the trick is quitted, or if the offender or her partner accidentally or purposely mixes the cards, the players abandon their hands, and the nonoffenders score 2 points. If the revoke is made against a lone hand, the lone player scores 4 points.

Cutthroat, or Three-Hand, Euchre

When three persons play, two persons play in temporary partnership against the maker of the trump. Scoring is the same as in basic euchre, but if the temporary partners euchre the maker of the trump, they each score two points.

Two-Hand Euchre

When two persons play, they strip the sevens and eights from the deck. All rules applying to the basic four-hand game of euchre apply to its two-hand variation.

Six-Hand Euchre

When six persons participate, three play against three, and the partners sit alternately around the table. If a lone hand prevails against three opponents, he scores game. Otherwise, scoring remains the same.

Railroad Euchre

Railroad euchre, a four-hand variation, differs from the basic game of euchre as follows:

1. The players use the joker, which ranks above the right bower. They also mutually select a trump suit in advance in case the joker is turned up as the proposed trump.

2. The player going it alone may, optionally, discard one card and call for her partner's best card. The partner responds and then lays her hand face down on the table during the play. Conversely, if the dealer's partner decides to go it alone, the dealer may give her partner a card from her hand or the turned-up trump, whichever she deems better.

3. Either opponent may also call for her partner's best card to go it alone against the first lone hand. Euchre of a lone hand by two opponents scores two points; euchre of one lone hand by another lone hand scores four points. Otherwise, the scoring remains the same.

4. Euchre enthusiasts often combine *Laps, Slams, Jambone,* and/or *Jamboree* with *Railroad Euchre* to form variations in the game.

Buck Euchre

Buck Euchre requires four players to use a 24-card deck, plus the joker; five players, a 28-card deck, plus the joker; six players, a 32-card deck, plus the joker. Apart from these basic requirements, *Buck Euchre* differs from regular euchre as follows:

1. Each person plays by and for himself in cutthroat fashion.

2. Before the deal, each player puts one chip in the pool, as agreed to at the start of the game.

3. The person ordering up or otherwise making the trump must take three tricks or put one chip in the pool for each trick he fails to take. Each trick taken is worth one chip. If a player takes all five tricks, he wins the entire pool.

Call-Ace Euchre

The rules governing the number of players, the kind of deck used, and the deal are the same in *Call-Ace Euchre* as in *Buck Euchre*. The differences between the two games are as follows:

1. The joker is not used.

2. The dealer turns up the trump, leaving three unknown cards in the four-hand game, two in the five-hand game, and one in the six-hand game.

3. The player who orders up or names the trump may call out the best card of any suit, except trumps, and the holder of that card becomes her partner. The partner, however, remains unknown until she plays the card called out. Since all cards are not in play, the best card might be a king, queen, or jack. It might be that the trump caller is holding that card herself, in

which case she would not have a partner. The trump caller also might say, "Alone," or call on a suit of which she holds the ace.

4. If the trump caller and her partner take three tricks, they win the hand and the game in a ten-minute game.

If the 5-, 7-, or 10-point game is being played, they each score 1 point; for a march, or five tricks, they each score three points. If they are euchred, each opponent scores two points. A lone hand scores one point for three tricks. For a march, the lone player scores one point for each person playing, including herself, in the game.

CHILDREN'S GAMES

Pig

This is a very hilarious game for children or for adults to play with children. Anybody can learn it in two or three minutes, and one extra minute makes you an expert!

Players: 3 to 13—5 or 6 makes the best game

Cards: Four of a kind for each player in the game. For example, five players would use 20 cards: four aces, four kings, four queens, four jacks, and four tens. For six players you would add the nines.

The Deal: Any player shuffles and deals four cards to each player.

To Win the Game: Get four of a kind in your own hand, or be quick to notice when somebody else gets four of a kind.

The Play: The players look at their cards to see if they were dealt four of a kind. If nobody has four of a kind, each player puts some unwanted card face down on the table and passes it to the player to the left, receiving a card at the same time from the player to the right.

If, still, nobody has four of a kind, each player once again passes a card to the left and gets a new card from the right.

The play continues in this way until one player gets four of a kind. That player stops passing or receiving cards. Instead, he puts his finger to his nose.

The other players must be quick to notice this, and each of them must stop passing in order to put a finger to his nose. The last player to put a finger to his nose is the "Pig."

Strategy: In trying to put together four of a kind, you usually start with a pair. For example, suppose you are dealt two kings, one queen, and one ace. Keep the two kings, and pass either the queen or the ace. As soon as you get another king, save all three of them, and pass your fourth card. Sooner or later your fourth king will come in.

Don't get so interested in looking for your own four of a kind that you are blind to what the other players are doing. Keep one eye on everybody else, particularly on those who look very eagerly at the cards they are receiving. The eager player probably has three of a kind and is just waiting for the fourth.

The best *Pig* player I know is a seven-year-old girl who doesn't try very hard to make four of a kind. She always tries to look excited, and talks and squeals as she gets each card, just as though she had three of a kind. While doing all this, she watches the other players to see which of them are most interested in her and which are interested in their own hands.

She knows that the players who are interested in *her* have *bad* hands, but that those who are thinking about the *game* have *good* hands. So little Lisa knows which players to watch, and she is never caught!

Concentration

Players: Any number at all—the more the merrier
Cards: 1 pack
The Deal: Spread the cards face down on a table. Don't bother to put them down neatly, but just jumble them up, making sure that no two cards overlap.

To Win the Game: Capture the largest number of cards.

The Play: Before play begins, the players should be told what their turn is, so that they know whether they are first, second, third, and so on.

The first player turns up any card and then turns up any other card. If the two cards match (for example, if they are two aces or two kings), the first player captures them as her pair. She then has another turn and proceeds to turn up two more cards in the hope of finding a pair. When she turns up two cards that are not a pair, she must turn them face down again in the same position. It now becomes the turn of the next player.

Strategy: The trick is to remember the cards that have been turned up and exactly where on the table they are. For example, suppose a player turns up a king and a ten. He has to turn those cards face down again. You do your best to remember exactly where that king is and where that ten is. Then, when it is your turn, you turn up a card on an entirely different part of the table, hoping to find another king or another ten. If you find another king, you can go right to the first king like a homing pigeon and you'll have a pair of kings to capture. If you find another ten, you can go right to the first ten and capture those cards, too.

If you try to remember too many cards, you may forget them all. It is much better to begin by trying to remember only two or three cards. When you find that you can do that easily, try remembering four cards. In this way you can gradually increase your skill until you can accurately remember the whereabouts of seven or eight cards at a time. This should be enough to win almost any game.

Slapjack

Slapjack is one of the most entertaining games that you can play with a deck of cards. It is one of the very first games my grandfather taught me, and he didn't complain when I won from him regularly.

Players: 2 to 8. The game is best for 3 or 4 players.

Cards: 1 pack

The Deal: One at a time to each player until all the cards have been dealt out. It doesn't matter if they don't come out even. The players square up their cards into a neat pile face down in front of them without looking at any cards.

To Win the Game: Win all the cards.

The Play: The player to the dealer's left begins by lifting the top card of her pile and dropping it face up in the middle of the table. The next player (to the left of the first player) does likewise—that is, he lifts the top card of his pile and drops it face up in the middle of the table, on top of the card that is already there. The play continues in this way, each player in turn lifting the top card of his pile and dropping it face up in the middle of the table.

As soon as any player turns up a jack, the fun begins. The first player to slap that jack wins the entire pile of cards in the middle of the table! If more than one player slaps at the jack, the one whose hand is at the bottom wins the pile.

This means that you have to keep your eyes open and be pretty quick to get your hand down on a jack. Sometimes your hand is pretty red when you're so quick that another player slaps your hand instead of the jack, but it's all in fun. Hopefully, grownups are careful not to play too roughly!

I used to beat my grandfather all the time because he would lift his hand high in the air before bringing it down on a jack, while I would swoop in sideways and could generally snatch the jack away before his hand even hit the table. Grandpa never seemed to learn!

Whenever you win cards, you must put them face down underneath the cards you already have.

The play goes on until one player has won all the cards. As soon as a player has lost his last card, he may watch for the next jack and try to slap it in order to get a new pile for himself. If he fails to get that next pile, he is out of the game. Sooner or later, all the players except one are "knocked out" in this way, and the cards all come to one player, who is the winner.

False Slaps: A player who slaps at a card that is *not* a jack must give the top card of her pile to the owner of the card that she slapped. If the false slapper has no cards to pay the penalty, she is out.

How to Turn Cards: At your turn to play you must lift the top card of your pile and turn it *away* from you as you drop it face up in the middle of the table. This is to make sure that you don't see the card before the other players do. Also, make sure that you let the card go as you drop it on the table.

Strategy: Naturally, you don't want the other players to have a big advantage, so turn the card over very quickly. Then you will see it just about as soon as they do.

Most players use the same hand for turning the cards and for slapping at jacks. It's a more exciting game, however, if you agree that the hand used for slapping will not be the same hand used for turning the cards.

Some players use the right hand to turn over the card with a quick motion, and they swoop down on the jack with the left hand. Other experts, since they are much swifter at swooping with the right hand, turn the card over with the left hand. You may have to try it both ways to see which is better for you.

The important thing to remember is that it's better to be a swift swooper than a slow slapper.

Snap

Players: 3 to 8—4 or 5 is best.
Cards: 1 pack
The Deal: Any player deals one card at a time, until all the cards have been dealt. They don't have to come out even.
To Win the Game: Win all the cards.
The Play: As in *Slapjack*, each player turns up one card at a time at his turn to play. The card must be turned away from the player and dropped on the table, except that each player starts a pile in front of himself for his turned-up cards. For example, in the game for four players, after each player has had a turn, there will be four piles of face-up cards and the four packs of cards face down that were dealt at the beginning.

When a player turns up a card that matches a face-up card on any other pile, the first player to say "Snap!" wins both piles and puts them face down under her own pack.

A player who says "Snap!" at the wrong time, when the turned-up card does not match one of the other piles, must give the top card of his pile to the player who just turned up her card.

As in *Slapjack*, a player who runs out of cards may stay in for the next "Snap!" in the hope of getting a new pile. If she does not win that "Snap," she is out. A player who cries a false "Snap" is out if he has no cards to pay the penalty.

Strategy: Players have to keep looking around to make sure they know which cards are on top of the piles, since these keep changing as the game goes on. They must be ready at all times to shout "Snap!" very quickly. If two or more players begin the word at the same time, the player who ends the word first wins. If you're a slow talker, this is no game for you.

My grandmother used to play this game with me. She preferred it to *Slapjack*—which can become rough. We had to make a special rule once because one little girl who was playing with us said "Snap!" every time a card was turned. She had to pay a penalty card most of the time, but this was more than offset because she won every single pile.

Grandma said this wasn't fair, so we adopted the rule that after three false "Snaps" a player was out.

War

Players: 2
Cards: 1 pack
To Win the Game: Win all the cards.
The Play: Each player puts his stack of cards face down in front of him and turns up the top card at the same time. The player who has the higher of the two turned-up cards wins both of them and puts them face down at the bottom of his stack of cards. The king is the highest card, and the ace is the lowest. The full rank of the cards is:

(Highest)  **(Lowest)**

Sometimes *War* is played with the ace high.

If the two turned-up cards are of the same rank, the players have a "war." Each turns one card face down and then one card face up. The higher of the two new face-up cards takes both piles (a total of six cards).

If the newly turned-up cards again match, there is *double war*. Each player once again turns one card face down and one card face up, and the higher of these two new face-up cards wins the entire pile of ten cards.

The game continues in this way until one player has all the cards.

This is a good game to play when you have a lot of time and nowhere to go.

War for Three

The Deal: When three players want to play *War*, take any card out of the deck and give 17 cards to each.

The Play: For the most part, the play is the same as in two-handed *War*, but when two cards turned up are the same, all three players join in the war by turning one card face down and one card face up. If two of the new turned-up cards are the same, all three players must once more turn one card down and one card face up. As usual, the highest card wins all cards that are used in the war.

If all three turned-up cards are the same, the players must engage in double war. Each player turns two cards face down and then one card face up. If the result is a tie, all three players engage in single war.

I Doubt It

Other Name: Cheat

Players: 3 or more

Cards: Use a single pack for 3 or 4 players. Shuffle   two packs together for 5 or more players.

The Deal: Two or three cards at a time are dealt so that each player gets an equal number of cards. When only a few cards are left, deal one at a time as far as the cards will go.

To Win the Game: Get rid of all your cards.

The Play: The player to the dealer's left puts from one to four cards face down in the middle of the table, announcing that she is putting down that number of aces. The next player puts down one to four cards and announces that he is putting down that number of deuces. The next player in turn does the same thing, stating that he is putting down that number of threes. The play proceeds in this sequence:

When any player puts down cards and makes his announce-

Starting Ending

ment, any other player may say, "I doubt it." The doubted cards must immediately be turned face up. If the statement was true, the doubter must take the entire pile into his hand. If the statement was false, the player who made the false statement must take the pile.

When the players are using two packs shuffled together, a player may put down any number of cards from one to eight.

When a player puts his last cards on the table, some other player must say, "I doubt it," since otherwise the game ends automatically. If the statement turns out to be true, the player wins the game.

A player who has no cards at all of the kind that she is supposed to put down is not allowed to skip her turn. She must put down one or more cards anyway and try to get away with her untruthful announcement. If somebody doubts her claim, she will have to pick up the pile.

If two or more participants say "I doubt it" at the same time, the one nearest the player's left wins the tie; that is, he picks up the pile if the statement turns out to be true after all.

Three-Card I Doubt It

The Deal: The cards are dealt out equally as far as they will go. Put any remaining cards face down in the middle of the table.

The Play: Each player in turn puts down exactly three cards. Instead of starting with aces automatically, the first player may choose any denomination at all. For example, she may say, "Three nines." The next player must say, "Three tens," and so on. When a player has one or two cards left, he must draw enough cards from those put face down in the middle of the table to make up a total of three.

Go Fish

Players: 2 to 5

Cards: 1 pack

The Deal: If only two play, deal seven cards to each. If four or five play, deal five cards to each. Put the rest of the pack face down on the table, forming the stock.

To Win the Game: Form more "books" than any other player. A book in this game is four of a kind, such as four kings, four queens, and so on.

The Play: The player to the dealer's left begins by saying to some other player, "(Jane), give me your *nines*." He *must* mention the name of the player he is speaking to, and he *must* mention the exact rank that he wants (aces, kings, queens, etc.), and he *must* have at least one card of the rank that he is asking for.

The player who is addressed must hand over all the cards he has in the named rank, but if he has none, he says, "Go fish!"

When told to "go fish," a player must draw the top card of the stock. The turn to ask then passes to the player to his left.

If a player succeeds in getting some cards when she asks for them, she keeps her turn and may ask again. She may ask the same player or some different player, and she may ask for any rank in her new question.

If a player who has been told to "go fish" picks a card of the rank he has asked for, he shows this card immediately before putting it into his hand, and his turn continues. (In some very strict games, a player's turn would continue only if the card he fished for completed a book for him.)

Upon getting the fourth card of a book, the player shows all four, places them on the table in front of him, and continues his turn.

If a player is left without cards, she may draw from the stock at her turn and ask for cards of the same rank as the card that she has drawn. After the stock has been used up, a player who has no cards is out of the game.

The game ends when all 13 books have been assembled. The player with the most books wins.

Strategy: When a player asks for cards and gets them but does not put down a completed book, you can tell that he has either two or three of that rank. For example, suppose John requests queens and gets one queen from the player he has asked. John does not put down a book of queens, but asks some new question and is told to "go fish." You now know that John held at least one queen to give him the right to ask for queens. He has received a queen, which gives him a total of either two or three queens.

In the same way, you know something about a player's hand

when she asks for a card and gets nothing at all. For example, suppose Laura asks somebody for nines and is told to "go fish" at once. You know that Laura must have at least one nine in her hand.

Little by little, you can build up information about the cards the other players are holding. If you know that another player has queens, but you have no queens yourself, the information does you no good. If you have a queen yourself, however, you are then allowed to ask for queens, and if you ask the right person because of the information you have, you may get as many as three cards and be able to put down an entire book in front of you.

Fish for Minnows

This is a simpler way of playing *Go Fish*, and it is especially good for very young players.

The Deal: Deal out all the cards, not worrying about it if they don't happen to come out even.

The Play: At his turn, a player asks for a rank, and the player who has been asked must hand over one such card, if he has one. The object is to form pairs instead of books of four. As soon as a player gets a pair, he puts them face down in front of him.

To Win the Game: Accumulate the most pairs.

Authors

Players: 2 to 5
Cards: 1 pack
This game is a lot like *Go Fish*, but it can be played very seriously and with great skill.
The Deal: All 52 cards are dealt out, even though they may not come out even.
The Play: At her turn, a player asks for a single card by naming both its rank and its suit. For example, she might say, "Bill, give me the jack of spades." Her turn continues if she gets the card she asked for, but it passes to the left as soon as she asks for a card that the player doesn't hold.
To Win the Game: Win more books (four cards of the same rank) than any other player.

Old Maid

Other Name: Queen of Spades
Players: 2 or more
Cards: 51, including only three of the four queens. Remove one queen from the pack before beginning the game.
The Deal: One card at a time is dealt to each player, as far as the cards will go. It doesn't matter if the cards don't come out even.
To Win the Game: Avoid getting "stuck" with the last unpaired queen.
The Play: Each player sorts his cards and puts aside, face down, all the cards that he can pair—two by two. For example, he might put aside two kings, two queens, two jacks, and so on.

If he had three queens and three jacks, he would be allowed to put two of them aside, but the third jack and third queen would stay in his hand.

After each player has discarded his paired cards, the dealer presents her cards, fanned out but face down, to the player at her left. The player at the left selects one card (blindly, since the hand is presented face down) and quickly examines it to see if it pairs some card still in his hand. If so, he discards the pair. In any case, this player now fans his cards out and presents them face down to the player at his left.

This process continues, each player in turn presenting his hand, fanned out and face down, to the player at the left. Eventually, every card will be paired except one of the three queens. The player who is left with the odd queen at the end of the hand is the "Old Maid."

Whenever a player's last card is taken, he drops out. He can no longer be the "Old Maid."

Strategy: *Old Maid* can be learned in about one minute, and nothing you can do will improve your chance of winning. The player who is stuck with an odd queen during the middle of the play usually looks worried and will often squeal with delight if the player to his left selects the queen. If you keep alert, you can usually tell which player at the table has an odd queen as the play is going on.

If you have the odd queen, put it somewhere in the middle of your hand when you present it to the player at your left. Most players tend to pick a card from the middle rather than the ends. Make use of this same principle to defend yourself if you think that the player at your right has the odd queen when he presents his hand for you to make your choice. He will usually put the queen in the middle somewhere, and you can usually avoid choosing it by taking one of the two end cards instead.

It isn't bad to get an odd queen toward the beginning of the play, for you will have many chances to get rid of it. It will then probably stay in some other player's hand or move only part of the way around the table.

If you like to cause a little confusion, act worried when you don't really have the queen in your hand. Another idea is to act delighted when the player to your left picks some perfectly harmless card. This will make the other players in the game believe that he has taken the odd queen from you. You yourself will usually know where the odd queen really is, but the other players may be in considerable doubt.

GAMES WITH STOPS

Sequence

Players: 2 to 10—4 or 5 players make the best game.
Cards: One at a time to each player until the deck is used up. It doesn't matter if some of the players are dealt more cards than the others.
To Win the Game: Get rid of all your cards.
The Play: The player to the dealer's left puts down his lowest card in any suit he chooses. The rank of the cards is:

(Highest) 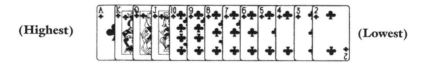 (Lowest)

After the first card has been put down on the table, whoever has the next highest card in the same suit must put it down. This process continues until somebody finally plays the ace of that suit.

For example, suppose the first player's lowest spade is the four. He puts the four of spades down on the table. Somebody else plays the five of spades, and another player puts down both the six and the seven of spades (it doesn't matter if the same person plays two or more cards in a row). This process continues until somebody finally plays the ace of spades.

When the ace is reached, the one who plays it must begin a new suit. As before, the player who begins the suit must begin with her lowest card in that suit.

Sooner or later, one of the players will get rid of all his cards. He wins the hand, and the other players lose one point for every card they still have when the hand comes to an end. (A simpler method is to forget the scoring by points and just play to win the hand.)

Strategy: Practically no skill is required for this game. It is wise, though, to begin with the deuce of some suit when it is your turn to begin a play. If you have no deuce, begin with a three, or with the lowest card of any suit in your hand. If you don't follow this policy, you may eventually get stuck with a deuce or a three in your hand.

The great value of this game for very young children is that it is very easy to teach and children get practice in recognizing numbers and learning how they follow each other in sequence. For especially young children, you may want to remove the picture cards from the deck and use only the cards from 1 to 10. In this case, of course, the ace is the lowest card, and the ten is the highest card of each suit.

Snip, Snap, Snorem

Players: 3 or more—the more the merrier
Cards: 1 pack
The Deal: One at a time to each player, until the entire pack is used up. It doesn't matter if some players have more cards than the others.
To Win the Game: Get rid of all your cards.
The Play: The player to the dealer's left puts any card face up on the table. The next player to the left matches the play with the same card in a different suit, saying "Snip." The next player to the left continues to match the original play with the same card in a third suit, saying "Snap." The next player follows with the fourth card of the same kind, saying "Snorem." If a player is unable to follow with a matching card, he says, "Pass," and his turn passes to the next player to the left.

For example, let's say the first player puts down a six of hearts. The next player to the left has no six and therefore must say "Pass." The next player has the six of diamonds and puts it down, saying "Snip." The next player to the left has both of the remaining sixes and therefore puts them down one at a time, saying "Snap" for the first one and "Snorem" for the second.

The player who says "Snorem," after putting down the fourth card of a kind, plays the first card of the next group of four. If he has more than one of a kind, he must put down as many as he has instead of holding out one of the cards for "Snorem." For example, if you have two kings, you must put both of them down if you decide to play a king. You are not allowed to put down just one of the kings and wait for the other two kings to appear before showing your remaining king for a "Snorem."

The first player to get rid of his cards wins the game.

Crazy Eights

Other Names: Rockaway
Players: 2 to 8. The game is best for two, three, or four. In the four-handed game, the players who sit across the table from each other are partners.
Cards: Seven to each player in a two-handed game Five to each player when more than two are playing.

The Deal: After the correct number of cards is dealt to each player, put the rest of the cards on the table face down as the stock. Turn the top card face up to begin another pile.

The Play: The player to the left of the dealer must match the card that has been turned up. That is, he must put down a card of the same suit or of the same rank.

For example, suppose the card first turned up is the nine of spades. The first player must put down either another spade or another nine.

The newly played card is placed on top of the turned-up card. It is up to the next player to match the new card either in suit or in rank.

The four eights are wild; that is, you may play an eight at any time, when it is your turn. When putting down an eight, you are allowed to call it any suit at all, as you please. For example, you might put down the eight of hearts and say "Spade." The next player would then have to follow with a spade.

If, at your turn, you cannot play, you must draw cards from the top of the stock until you are able to play or until there are no more cards left. You are allowed to draw cards from the stock, at your turn, even if you are able to play *without* drawing. This is sometimes a good idea.

To Win the Game: Get rid of all your cards. The first player to get rid of all his cards wins.

Sometimes a hand ends in a block with nobody able to play, and with nobody having played out. The hand is then won by the player with the smallest number of cards. If two or more players tie for this honor, the hand is declared a tie.

Strategy: The most important principle is not to play an eight too quickly. If you waste an eight when you are not really in trouble, you won't have it to save you when the going gets tough.

The time that you really need an eight to protect yourself is when you have been *run out of a suit*. For example, after several spades have been played, you might not be able to get another spade even if you drew every single card in the stock. If you are also unable to match the rank of the card that has been put down, you may be forced to pick up the entire stock before your turn is over. From here on, of course, it will be very hard for you to avoid a disastrous defeat. An eight will save you from this kind of misfortune, since you can put it down in place of a spade, and you may be able to call a suit that does for your opponent what the spade would have done for you!

If you're lucky, you won't have to play an eight at the beginning, and you can save it to play as your last card. If you're not quite as lucky as this, it is sensible to play the eight as your next to last card. With a little luck, you will then be able to play your last card when your next turn comes—and win the hand. To play an eight with more than two cards in your hand is seldom wise. It is usually better to draw a few cards from stock in order to find a playable card.

The best way to beat an opponent is to run her out of some

suit. If you have several cards in one suit, chances are your opponent will be short in that suit. As often as you get the chance, keep coming back to your long suit until your opponent is unable to match your card. Eventually, she will have to draw from stock and may have to load herself up badly before she is able to play.

Hollywood Eights

Equipment: Paper and pencil for scoring

This is the same as the original game of *Crazy Eights*, except that a score is kept in points with pencil and paper. When a hand comes to an end, each loser counts up his cards as follows:

Each eight	50
Each king, queen, jack, or ten	10
Each ace	1
Each other card	its face value

The winner of a hand gets credit for the total of all points lost by the other players.

For example, suppose you have an eight, a nine, and a seven when a hand ends. The eight counts 50 points, the nine counts 9, and the seven counts 7. The total is 50 + 9 + 7, or 66 points.

Hollywood scoring: Three separate game scores are kept. The first time a player wins a hand, his score is credited to him in the first game score. The second time a player wins a hand, he gets credit for his victory both in the first game and also in the second game. The third time a player wins, his score is credited to him in all three games. He continues to get credit in all three games from then on.

Sometimes the game runs on until everybody feels like stopping. In this case, the three game scores are added whenever everybody wants to stop. The winner is the player with the biggest total for the three scores.

Suppose you win five hands in a row, with scores of 10, 25, 40, 20, and 28 points. Your score would look like this:

FIRST GAME		SECOND GAME		THIRD GAME	
	10		25		40
(+25)	35	(+40)	65	(+20)	60
(+40)	75	(+20)	85	(+28)	88
(+20)	95	(+28)	113		
(+28)	123				

100 Scoring: A more popular method is to end a game as soon as any player's score reaches 100. When this happens in the first of the three games, the other two games continue. In the later hands, the score is entered on the second game and third games, but no further entry is made in the finished first game. Sooner or later, some player reaches a score of 100 in the second game, and this likewise comes to an end. Eventually, also, some player reaches a score of 100 in the third game, and then all three games have ended.

The winner is the player with the highest total score when all three game scores have been added up.

Go Boom

Players: 2 or more
Cards: 1 pack
The Deal: Seven cards are dealt to each player. The rest of the pack is put face down in the middle of the table.
To Win the Game: Get rid of all your cards.
The Play: The player to the left of the dealer puts any card on the table. The next player to her left must follow by matching the suit or rank of that card. Each player in turn after this must match the previous card in suit or rank.

For example, suppose the first player puts down the jack of diamonds. The next player may follow with any diamond or with another jack. If the second player decides to follow with the jack of clubs, the third player may then match with a club or with one of the two remaining jacks.

When a player cannot match the previous card, he must draw cards from the stock until he is able to play. If a player uses up the stock without finding a playable card, he may say "Pass," and his turn passes to the next player.

When everybody at the table has had the chance to play or say "Pass," the cards are examined to see who has played the highest card. The cards rank as follows:

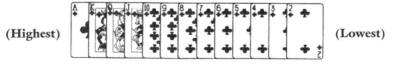

(Highest)   (Lowest)

The player who put down the highest card has the right to begin the next play. If there is a tie for first place among cards of the same rank, the card that was played first is considered higher.

The play continues in this way until one player gets rid of all her cards. That player wins the hand.

If none of the players is very young, you might want to use a system of point scoring. When a hand comes to an end, each loser counts the cards left in his hand as follows:

Each picture card	10
Each ace	1
Each other card	its face value

The winner of the hand is credited with the total of all points lost by the other players.

Strategy: The strategy in *Go Boom* is much the same as in *Crazy Eights*. You try to run your opponent out of a suit in hopes that he will not be able to match your play with a card of the same suit or the same rank.

In the early stages of play, it is useful to play as high a card as possible in order to have the best chance to win the privilege of beginning the next play.

Fan-Tan

Other Names: Card Dominoes, Sevens, Parliament
Players: 3 to 8
Equipment: A bunch of counters—poker chips, matchsticks, toothpicks, dried beans, etc.

The Deal: One card at a time to each player until all the cards have been dealt. It doesn't matter if some players get more cards than others. Give an equal number of counters to each player.

To Win the Game: Get rid of all your cards.

The Play: To open, the player to the left of the dealer must play any seven, if possible. If not, the first player with a seven opens. After the seven is played, the next player to the left may play a seven or any card in the same suit and in sequence with the card previously played.

For example, suppose that the player to the dealer's left put the seven of spades on the table. The next player may put down a new seven or may play the eight of spades so that it covers half of the seven of spades. The second player, instead, might have chosen to play the six of spades, putting it down also so that it just covered half of the seven of spades. If the eight of spades were played, the next player would have the right to put down the nine of spades. If the nine of spades were played, the next player would have the right to put down the ten of spades.

This process continues. At any turn, a player may put down a new seven or may continue a sequence that builds up in suit from a seven to a king or down from a seven to an ace. The king is the highest card that may be played on a sequence and the ace is the lowest. If a player does not have an appropriate card, he must put a counter into the middle of the table.

The play continues until one player gets rid of all his cards. That player then collects all the counters in the middle of the table. In addition, each loser pays out one counter for every card left in her hand.

Strategy: It is usually easy to get rid of cards of middle size, such as eights, nines, sixes, and fives. It is usually hard to get rid of very low or very high cards, such as aces and deuces or queens and kings.

The best tactic is to force the other players to build up to your high cards or down to your low cards. You can't always carry it off, but you can try.

If you have the eight of spades, nobody can play the nine of spades or any higher spade until you have first put down your eight. If a player who has high spades finds no chance to play them, he must play something else at his turn. This other play may be just what you need to reach your own very low cards or your own very high cards.

This shows you the general strategy. Play as much as possible in the suit that will lead to your very high cards or to your very low ones. Wait as long as possible before playing in the suits in which you have only middle-rank cards. With just a little luck, you will get rid of your very high cards and your very low cards fairly early. You will then be able to get rid of your middle-rank cards in the last suit, catching the other players while they still have the very high and very low cards in that suit.

Liberty Fan-Tan

This is the same game as *Fan-Tan*, except that it isn't necessary to begin a suit by playing the seven. Nobody can start a new suit until the previous suit has been finished.

The player to the left of the dealer begins by playing any card of any suit. The next player must follow with the next-higher card in the same suit or must put one counter in the middle of the table. The third player must continue with the next card in sequence or must put one counter in the middle of the table. This process continues, building up past the king with the ace, deuce, and so on, until all 13 cards of the suit have been played. The one who plays the thirteenth card of the first suit may begin with any card in a new suit. Then the same process continues with a second suit.

The first player to get rid of all her cards takes all the counters from the pool.

Strategy: Your chance of winning is best when you can determine which suit will be played last. If you have very few cards in this suit, you have an excellent chance to win all the counters since you will get rid of your cards while the other players still have cards of that suit left.

The time to choose the last suit does not come after the third suit has been played, since at that point there is no choice. The choice is made after the second suit has been played, since then two suits remain. The player who chooses the third suit automatically fixes the other suit as the fourth.

If you happen to end the second suit, by good luck, you will then begin the play of the third. Naturally, you should play your longer suit, saving your shorter suit for last.

If the two suits are almost equal in length, it is sometimes wiser to play the shorter suit third and save the other suit for the last. The time to do this is when you have two cards in sequence in the shorter suit. If you start with the higher of these two cards, you will naturally be the one to finish the suit when you play the lower card.

For example, suppose you have a hand with spades:

You notice that the nine and the eight are in sequence.

Following the principle just mentioned, you would begin the suit by playing the nine. Other players would follow with the ten, jack, and queen, allowing you to play the king. Then someone would play the ace and you would follow with the two. The others would then play on until your eight would complete the suit. Having completed the suit, it is up to you to start the next suit, and this is exactly what you had in mind.

Use the same strategy of starting the second suit with the higher card if you have two cards in sequence. This will allow you to end the second suit and choose the third.

Commit

Players: 4 or more
Cards: 1 pack
Equipment: A bunch of counters—poker chips, matchsticks, toothpicks, dried beans, etc.
The Deal: Remove the eight of diamonds from the pack. Deal the cards one at a time as far as they will go evenly. Put the remaining cards face down in the middle of the table. Give an equal number of counters to each player.
To Win the Game: Get rid of all your cards.
The Play: The player to the dealer's left may put any card down on the table. She and the other players can then build up in sequence in the same suit.

For example, suppose Gina begins with the seven of clubs. Any player who has the eight of clubs puts it face up on the table. Then it is the turn of any player who has the nine of clubs. This continues until someone plays the king of clubs or until the sequence is stopped because the next card is one of those face down in the middle of the table—or the eight of diamonds, which has been removed.

When the play stops for either of these reasons, the person who played last begins a new sequence with any card in his hand.

The nine of diamonds is a special card in this game. You can of course play it when you end a sequence and it is your turn to begin a new one. But you can also play it in the middle of any sequence. When the nine of diamonds is played, each player in turn has the chance to proceed either with the ten of diamonds—continuing the diamond sequence—or with the sequence that was interrupted by the nine of diamonds.

For example, suppose Avery begins a sequence with the three of spades. Barbara puts down the four of spades and then follows it with a nine of diamonds. Chris, the player to the left, then has a choice to make. She may continue with a ten of diamonds, or go back to the five of spades. If she has neither card, the turn passes on to the left until somebody plays either the ten of diamonds or the five of spades, which determines how the sequence will continue.

When you play the nine of diamonds, you collect two counters from every player in the game. If anyone gets rid of all his cards before you have played the nine of diamonds, you must *pay* two counters to every player in the game.

When a player wins the game (by playing all his cards), the remaining players must show their hands. Any player who has a king must pay one counter to every other player in the game.

Strategy: As in the game of *Newmarket,* the best strategy is to begin with your lowest card in your longest suit.

It is helpful to remember the stops. At the beginning of a hand, the only stop you are sure of is the eight of diamonds. It pays to begin with a low diamond if you have the seven of diamonds in your hand, for then you will probably build up to that seven and have the chance to begin the next sequence.

Rolling Stone

Players: 4 to 6

Cards: When four people play, use the ace, king, queen, jack, ten, nine, eight, and seven of each suit. If there is a fifth player, add the sixes and fives. If there is a sixth player, add the fours and threes. There must be eight cards for each player.

The Deal: One card at a time until each player has eight cards. This uses up the pack.

To Win the Game: Get rid of all your cards.

The Play: The player to the dealer's left begins by putting down any card he pleases. Then the play moves to the left and the next player puts down another card in the same suit. The turns continue, always moving to the left, with the other players following with another card of the same suit, if they can, playing high or low, as they please.

When a player cannot put down a card of the same suit when it is her turn to play, she must pick up all the cards previously played in that sequence. This ends the trick, and the player who picks up the cards then begins the next trick by leading with any card she chooses.

The process continues. In most games a player picks up the cards several times. Eventually, one player will get rid of all his cards, and win the hand.

For the purpose of winning a trick, the cards rank as follows:

(Highest) 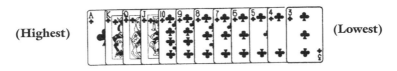 (Lowest)

Play or Pay

Players: 3 or more

Equipment: A handful of counters—poker chips, matchsticks, toothpicks, dried beans, etc,

The Deal: One card at a time to each player, until the pack has been used up. It doesn't matter if some players get more cards than others. Give an equal number of counters to each player.

To Win the Game: Get rid of all your cards.

The Play: The player to the left of the dealer may put down any card from her hand. The player to her left must follow with the next-highest card in the same suit—or must put a counter into the middle of the table. This process continues, with each player in turn either putting down the next card or paying one counter.

 and so on

The cards in their proper sequence is illustrated below.

The player who puts down the thirteenth card of a suit makes the first play in the next suit.

Keep on playing until someone wins by getting rid of all his cards. Each player then puts one counter in the middle of the table for each card left in his hand. The winner takes all the counters from the middle of the table.

Strategy: There is no skill in following suit; you either have the card or you don't. The only skill is in choosing the right card with which to begin a play.

If you have two cards in sequence in any suit, begin with the one that is higher in rank. Eventually, you will end that suit by playing the lower card of the sequence. This will give you the right to begin the next suit.

When possible, try to get rid of your long suits first.

CASSINO GAMES

Games of the Cassino variety (sometimes referred to as *Casino*) have been popular with adults and children for hundreds of years.

Cassino

Players: 2 to 4—best for 2

Cards: 1 pack

The Deal: The deck of 52 cards is used up in six deals. In the first deal:

The non-dealer receives two cards face down.

Then two cards are put face up on the table.

Then the dealer gives himself two cards face down.

And the process repeats, so that each player and the table have four cards each. In the remaining five deals, the dealer continues to give each player four cards—two at a time—but does not give any additional cards to the table.

The Play: Beginning with the non-dealer, each player in turn must play one card from her hand, until all four of her cards are gone. If she can find no better use for it, she simply lays her card face up on the table. This is called *trailing*. Whenever she can, though, she uses her card to capture cards from the table.

To Win the Game: Get the highest number of points. You get points by capturing the most cards, the most spades, the aces, the ten of diamonds *(Big Cassino)*, and the two of spades *(Little Cassino)*. See "Scoring."

Pairing: You may win cards in various ways. The simplest is by pairing. You may capture a card on the table by another of the same rank from your hand—a five with a five, and jack with a jack, and so on.

With a picture card—a jack, queen, or king—you may capture only one card, but with a card of lower rank you may take two or three of the same kind at the same time. If there are two sevens on the table and you have a seven in your hand, for example, you can take all three sevens.

Each player keeps captured cards in a pile, face down.

Building: All the lower cards, ace to ten, may be captured by building. Ace counts as 1. Each other card counts as its own value. Cards on the table may be taken in by higher cards to equal their sum.

For example, you may take a five and a two with a seven—or an ace and a nine with a ten. You may, at the same time, take additional cards by pairing. Suppose that the cards on the table are nine, eight, five, four, ace. You could take them all with a single nine, since the nines pair, eight and one make nine, and five and four make nine.

Leaving a Build: Suppose you have eight and three in your hand and there is a five on the table. You may put the three on the five and say, "Building an eight." Your intention is to capture the build with your eight on your next turn. You cannot build and capture in the same turn, because you are allowed to play only one card from your hand at a time.

If your opponent has an eight, she can capture your build. That is the risk of leaving a build. Yet the risk is usually worth taking, because in building, you make it harder for your opponent to capture the cards. She cannot take the five or the three by pairing or by making a build of her own.

Of course, you may not leave a build unless you have a card in your hand that can take it. You *are*, however, allowed to duplicate your build before taking it in. Suppose you have two eights in your hand. After building five and three, you could on your next turn simply put one eight on the build, and take it with the other eight on your third turn.

Or suppose after you build the five and three, your opponent trails a six, and you have a pair in your hand (besides the eight). You may take your two and put it—with the six—on the five-three build and wait until your next turn to take the duplicated build.

An important rule is that when you have left a build on the table, you must deal with it at your next turn—take it in—or increase or duplicate it. You are not allowed to trail or to take in other cards instead.

Increasing a Build: Suppose your opponent has laid a four from her hand on a five on the table and called out, "Building nine." You have an ace and a ten. You may add the ace to her build and say, "Building ten." You are allowed to increase a build of your own, in the same way.

But there are two restrictions on increasing a build. First, you may increase only a *single* build, such as the five-four, not one that has been duplicated in any way, such as five-four-nine. Second, the card you use to increase it must come from your hand; you are not allowed to use a card from the table.

Scoring: After the last card of the sixth deal is played, any cards remaining on the table go to the player who was last to capture cards. Then each player looks through his captured cards and counts his score, as follows:

	points
Cards, for winning 27 or more cards	3
Spades, for winning seven or more spades	1
Big Cassino, the ten of diamonds	2
Little Cassino, the two of spades	1
Aces, each counting 1, total	4
	11

The first one to reach a total of 21 or more points wins.

RUMMY GAMES

Rummy is the most widely played of all card games. Many different forms of the game are played, but all have a very strong family resemblance. Once you have learned to play the basic game, you can pick up any variation in a few minutes.

Basic Rummy

Players: 2 to 6
Cards: 10 each when 2 play
      7 each when 3 or 4 play
      6 each when 5 or 6 play
Equipment: Pencil and paper for keeping score
The Deal: Deal the appropriate number of cards to each player and then put the rest of the cards face down in the middle of the table, forming the stock. Turn the top card face up, starting the discard pile.

In a two-handed game, the winner of each hand deals the next hand. When more than two play, the turn to deal passes to the left exactly as the cards are dealt out.

To Win the Game: Win points from your opponents. You usually keep track of these points with a pencil-and-paper score.

In order to win points, you must match up your cards. One way to match is to get three or four of a kind. For example, you might have three kings or four 10s, and so on.

A second way to match is to get sequences—cards that are next to each other in rank and are in the same suit. The rank of the cards in *Rummy* is:

(Highest) 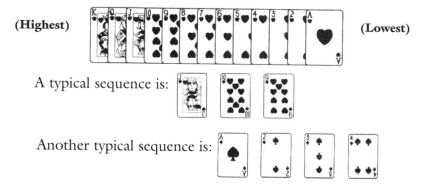 **(Lowest)**

A typical sequence is:

Another typical sequence is:

You need at least three cards for a sequence.

The Play: Each player at the table plays in turn, beginning with the player to the dealer's left. During your turn to play, you do three things:

You draw.
You meld (if you wish to do so).
You discard.

When you draw, you may pick up the top card of the stock or the top card of the discard pile. You add this card to your hand.

You *meld* by putting a group of matched cards down on the table. For example, you might put down three of a kind or four of a kind, or a sequence. You might even put down two groups of matched cards, if you are lucky enough to have them in your hand. You are not required to expose your meld if you don't wish to do so. You can keep it in your hand.

After some other player has melded, you may add to his meld when it's your turn. For example, if some player has put down three kings, you may add the fourth king at your turn to play. If some player has put down the six, seven, and eight of diamonds, you may add the nine and ten of diamonds, or just the nine or the five or five and four, or any such card or group of cards. You may add to a meld that has been put down previously by any player at the table—including your-self.

After you have drawn and melded (or after you have declined to meld), it is your turn to discard. You take any card from your hand and put it on top of the face-up pile in the middle of the table. This completes your play.

When, at your turn to play, you manage to meld all your cards, you win the game. You must begin your play with a draw, thus adding one card to your hand, and then you must meld either all the cards in your hand or all but one. If you meld all but one, that last card is your discard.

If no player has melded all his cards (called *going out*) by the time the stock is used up, the next player may take either the top card of the discard pile or the top card of the new stock that has been formed by turning the discard pile over. In either case, play continues as before until somebody does go out.

Scoring: The winner of a hand scores points by counting up the hands of all the other players in the game. Each loser counts his cards according to the following scale:

Picture cards—10 points each
Aces —1 point each
Other cards —their face value

A loser does not count cards that he has previously melded on the table, but he does count any cards that remain in his hand—*whether or not these cards match!*

A player goes "rummy" when he melds all his cards in one turn, without previously melding or adding to anybody else's meld. A player may go rummy by melding all his cards after the draw, or he may meld all but one and then discard that last card. Whenever a player goes rummy, he wins double the normal amount from each of the other players.

A score is kept on paper with a column for each player in the game. Whenever a player wins a hand, the amounts that he wins from the other players are put into his winning column.

Some players agree on a stopping time when they play *Rummy.* The winner of the game is the player who has the highest score when the agreed-upon time comes.

Other players end a game when any player reaches a certain total score, such as 500 points.

The score for each player is added up at the end of each hand.

Strategy: In all games of the *Rummy* family, you try to build up your hand by keeping cards that match and by discarding cards that do not match.

For example, if you drew the ten of spades, you would tend to keep it if your hand contained one or more tens, or the jack of spades or the nine of spades. In such cases, your ten of spades might be a useful card. Even if it did not immediately give you a meld, it would probably bring you closer to one.

If you drew a card that did not match anything in your hand, you would either discard it immediately or wait for a later chance to discard it.

If the player to your left picks a card from the discard pile, this gives you a clue to his hand. If, for example, he picks up the nine of diamonds, you know that he must have other nines or other diamonds in the neighborhood of the nine. If convenient, you would avoid throwing another nine or another diamond in that vicinity onto the discard pile. This is called playing *defensively*. You don't need to bother with defensive play against anybody but the player to your left, since your discard would be covered up by the time any *other* player wanted to draw.

The advantage of melding is that you cannot lose the value of those cards even if some other player wins the hand.

The advantage of holding a meld in your hand is that nobody can add to the meld while it is still in your hand. A second advantage is the possibility of going rummy all in one play.

It sometimes pays to hold up a meld, but most successful *Rummy* players make it a habit to put melds down fairly quickly. It is usually safe to hold up a meld for one or two turns, but after that it becomes dangerous. If another player goes out before you have melded, you will lost those matched cards just as though they were unmatched.

Contract Rummy

Other Name: Liverpool Rummy
Players: 3 to 8
Cards: 2 packs of 52 cards plus one joker, for 3
      or 4 players
Equipment: Paper and pencil for keeping score
The Deal: Deal ten cards to each player, except in Deal 7, when each player receives 12. Put the rest of the cards face down in the middle of the table, forming the stock. Turn the top card of the stock face up beside it, starting the discard pile.
To Win the Game: Get rid of all the cards in your hand by melding them.
Melds: The melds are as in *Basic Rummy. Groups* of three or four cards of the same rank, like queens; *sequences* of three or more cards of the same suit, as shown below:

The Contract: A game consists of seven deals. In each deal, a player's first meld must be a combination of two or three sets according to this schedule:

Deal 1: two groups
Deal 2: one group and one sequence
Deal 3: two sequences
Deal 4: three groups
Deal 5: two groups and a sequence
Deal 6: one group and two sequences
Deal 7: three sequences

When you meld in Deals 1–6, you may put down only three cards per set. If you have additional matching cards, you may put them down at any later turn.

In Deal 7, however, you must meld all 12 cards at once, thus going out.

The Play: As in *Basic Rummy*, a turn consists of a draw, melding (if you wish), and a discard.

If you, the first player, decide not to draw the top card of the discard pile, you must say so. Then any other player who wants it may take it. If two or more want it, the person nearest you (to the left) is entitled to it. He must pay for the privilege of taking the discard out of turn, though, by drawing the top card of the stock also. He must then await his regular turn before melding or discarding. Then you resume your turn, drawing the top card of the stock.

Your first meld of any kind must be the *contract*. After that, you are not allowed to meld any new sets, but you may add matching cards to any sets on the table—yours and the other players'.

A peculiarity of the game is that a sequence may be built to the ace both ways, making a set of 14 cards. (Of course, this rarely happens.)

Wild Cards: The joker is wild. You may call it any card you please, to help you get rid of cards by melding. You must say, though, what card it represents. For example, if you put the joker down with the seven of spades and the seven of diamonds, you must say either "seven of hearts" or "seven of clubs." The reason for this is shown by the next rule. A player who holds the named card may, in her turn, put it down in place of the joker, thus getting the joker for her own use.

Many players like to have additional wild cards, to make it easier to form sets for the contract. Deuces are often used as wild, but a deuce cannot be captured, as a joker can. However, if a deuce is melded in a sequence, any player may put the natural card in its place and move the deuce to either end of the sequence.

Ending Play: Play continues until somebody goes out. If the stock is exhausted, the discard pile is turned over without shuffling.

Scoring: The player who goes out scores zero—which is good! Each other player scores the total of the cards left in his hand. Aces and wild cards count 15 each, picture cards are 10, other cards count their face value. The player with the *lowest* total score after Deal 7 wins the game.

Knock Rummy

Players: 2 to 6
Cards: 10 cards to each player when 2 play
7 cards to each player when 3 or 4 play
5 cards to each player when 5 or 6 play
Equipment: Paper and pencil for keeping score
The Play: The play follows *Basic Rummy*, but there is no melding until somebody knocks. To "knock" means to lay down your whole hand face up, ending the play. You may knock in your turn, after drawing but before discarding. You do not have to have a single meld to knock—but you had better be convinced that you have the low hand.

When anybody knocks, all players lay down their hands,

arranged in such melds as they have, with the *unmatched* cards separate. What counts is *the total of unmatched* cards.

If the knocker has the lowest count, he wins the difference of counts from each other player.

If he lays down a *rum hand*—one with no unmatched card—he wins an extra 25 points from everybody, besides the count of unmatched cards held by the others.

If somebody beats or ties the knocker for low count, that player wins the difference from everybody else.

When the knocker is beaten, he pays an extra penalty of 10 points.

It's best to keep score with paper and pencil. Each item should be entered twice—*plus* for the winner and *minus* for the loser.

Gin Rummy

Gin is one of the best and also one of the most popular of the *Rummy* games.

Player: 2
Cards: A regular pack of 52. The ranking is:

(Highest)  (Lowest)

Equipment: Paper and pencil for keeping score
The Deal: Each player receives ten cards, dealt one at a time. Place the rest of the deck face down in the middle of the table

to form the stock. Turn over the top card of the stock beside it. This *upcard* starts the discard pile.

The Play: The non-dealer plays first. If she wants the upcard, she may take it, but if she doesn't want it, she must say so without drawing. Then the dealer may take the upcard, if he wishes, and discard one card from his hand, face up. After he has taken or refused it, the non-dealer continues with her turn, drawing one card—the top card of the stock or the new top of the discard pile. Then she must discard one card face up on the discard pile. The turns alternate and there are no further complications.

To Win the Game: Reduce the count of your unmatched cards.

A "matched set" in *Gin* is the same as a "meld" in *Basic Rummy*—three or four cards of the same rank, or three or more cards in sequence in the same suit. For example, here are two matched sets:

Since in *Gin,* aces rank low:

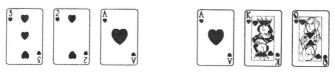

The three cards on the left are a sequence. Those on the right are not.

The point values are:

Ace: 1
Picture cards: 10
Other cards: face value

Knocking: All melding is kept in the hand until some player brings matters to a halt by laying down all his ten cards either by "ginning" or by "knocking."

To gin, you lay down all your cards in melds. When you knock, you have unmatched cards whose total is ten or less. You may knock only when it is your turn to play, after drawing and before discarding. The final discard is made *face down*, thereby indicating the intention to knock. If you simply place the card face up, intending to lay down your hand, you could be stopped, because—according to the rules—the face-up discard ended your turn.

As you play, you arrange your cards in matched sets with the unmatched cards to one side. It is customary to announce the total count of your unmatched cards by saying something like, "Knocking with five," or "I go down for five." Your opponent then exposes her hand, arranged by matched sets and unmatched cards. She is entitled to lay off cards on your sets, provided that you don't have a *gin hand*—all ten cards matched.

Knock hand

For example, if you had the hand shown above, your opponent could lay off the fourth jack, and the ten and six of hearts, if she had any of these cards.

Scoring: Your opponent counts her remaining unmatched cards, after laying off what she can on your hand. If this count is higher than yours, you win the difference. If your opponent has the same count that you have—or a lower one—she scores the difference (if any), plus 25 points for *undercutting* you.

If you lay down a gin hand, your opponent may not lay off any cards on it. You win the opponent's count, plus a bonus of 25 points. This bonus cannot be won when you knock. Suppose, for example, you play 'possum with a gin hand until your opponent knocks with one point or more. You would win her count, plus 25 for undercutting, but you don't get the bonus for a gin hand.

Keeping Score: Keep score with pencil and paper. Enter the net result of a hand in the column under the winner's name, draw a line below the item, and then write the running total. The lines between items are important, to keep track of how many hands were won by each player.

The first player to reach a total of 100 or more wins the game. You score a bonus of 100 for winning and an additional 100 for a *shutout*—also called "whitewash," "skunk," "Schneider," "goose-egg," etc.—if your opponent has not scored a single point. Then each player is credited with 25 points for each winning hand. This is called the *line* or *box* score. The winner then carries forward the difference between his own grand total and his opponent's.

500 Rummy

The chief feature of *500 Rummy* is that you score for melding as well as for going out.

Other Name: Sequence Dummy
Players: 3 to 8
Cards: When more than 4 play, use 2 packs of 52 shuffled together.
Equipment: Paper and pencil for keeping score
The Deal: Seven cards go to each player. The turn to deal passes to the left.

The Play: As in *Basic Rummy*, you may begin your turn by drawing the top card of the stock or the discard pile. But you have a third choice: You may draw any card of the discard pile, no matter how deeply it is buried, provided that you immediately meld this card. You must also pick up all the cards that cover it and add them to your hand. You then proceed to meld all the cards you wish to. Your turn ends when you discard.

Discards are not stacked in a pile as in most *Rummy* games, but are spread out in an overlapping fan so that all the cards can be seen. It is of course important not to mix up the order in which they lie. When you "dig deep" into the discards, courtesy requires that you leave the cards on the table for a while, to give the other players a chance to see what you're getting.

Melds are made as in *Basic Rummy*. You may add cards to your own melds and also to those belonging to other players.

Play ends when some player gets rid of all his cards, with or without making a final discard. If nobody goes out by the time the stock is exhausted, play continues so long as each player in turn draws from the discard pile, but it ends as soon as any player fails to do so.

Scoring: When play ends, each player counts up the difference between the cards he has melded and the cards left in his hand. This difference (which may be plus or minus) is added to his running total score, which is kept on paper.

The cards count as follows:

Ace	15 or 1, if it was melded in
a low sequence	
Picture cards	10 each
Other cards	face value

The first player to score 500 points wins the game.

Strategy: Much more is won by melding than by going out. Try to meld as much as possible, and to meld high cards rather than low ones. For this purpose, you'll want to get as many cards into your hand as you can. The deeper you have to dig into the discard pile, the happier you'll be!

If you are dealt a low meld, such as three deuces, discard one of them as soon as you can. Then, after the discard pile has grown to 10 or 12 cards, reclaim your deuce to meld it—and get some booty! Just don't be too greedy; if you wait too long, somebody else may take the pile, for you can be sure that the others will "salt" the pile too, if they have the chance.

At the beginning of a game, try to avoid making it too easy for another player to take the discard pile. You may make it easy if you discard a card that pairs with another already in the pile, or that is in suit and sequence with one in the pile. Of course, there comes a time when you have no more safe discards. Then follow the principle of doing the least damage. Discard a card that may let another player take a few cards, rather than a great many.

As a rule, don't meld unless you have to in order to dig into the discard pile. Keeping a meld of high cards in your hand, especially aces, puts the fellow who has the fourth ace on the spot. If he discards it, he gives you a chance to pick up the pile; if he holds it, he may get stuck with it. If you meld your aces, his troubles are over. If you are too lavish in melding, you may help another player go out.

You need to be quick to switch your tactics, however, when the stock is nearly gone or when another player reduces his hand to only a few cards. That's the time to meld your high cards, to be sure that they will count for you instead of against you.

A trump suit is one that is given a special privilege: it can take all the other suits. For example, if spades are trumps, a spade will win over any heart, club, or diamond. The deuce of spades then can take the ace of hearts, although the ace of hearts can win over any lower heart.

In some games, the trump suit is determined by turning up a card from the deck—its suit becomes trump. In other games, the right to name the trump suit is decided by the players *bidding*. It goes to the player who is willing to pay most for that right. Players *bid* what they are willing to pay—a number of counters to be put in a pool, for example. Usually, each bidder names a number of points or tricks that she hopes to win. The one who names the trump must win at least what she has bid, in order to advance her score. If she fails, points are taken away from her or her opponent's score (according to the particular game). Failing to make a bid goes by different names in different games—"set," "euchre," "bate," and so on.

TRUMP GAMES

Linger Longer

A good way to start learning trump games.

Players: 4 to 6

Cards: Each player receives as many cards as there are players in the game. For example, with five players, each receives five cards.

The Deal: The last card dealt, which goes to the dealer, is shown to all the players. It decides the trump suit for that trick. The rest of the deck is placed face down in the middle of the table, forming the stock.

The Play: The player to the left of the dealer makes the first *lead* (play), putting down in the middle of the table any card in the trump suit, if he can. Otherwise, he may put down whatever card he pleases. The other players must *follow suit*, putting down any cards in their hand that match the suit of the first lead.

The cards are played in "tricks." Each player tries to capture the trick of four cards by playing the highest trump, or, if there is no trump, by the highest card played of the suit that was led.

When a player wins a trick, he "owns" those cards and draws the top card of the stock. That card determines the trump suit for the next trick. When a player is left without any cards, he has to drop out of the game, and the others play on.

To Win the Game: Get all the cards and be the last player left when everyone else has dropped out. If two or more players are down to one card each at the end, the winner of the last trick wins the game.

Napoleon

Other Name: Nap
Players: 2 to 6
Cards: A regular pack of 52
Equipment: A handful of counters—poker chips,
                   matchsticks, toothpicks, dried beans, etc.

The Deal: Each player receives five cards, one at a time. Give out the counters, the same number to each player.

The Bidding: The player to the left of the dealer has the first turn. He *bids* (predicts) the number of tricks he will take if he is allowed to name the trump suit. Each player has one turn in which he may pass or may bid from one to five. A bid of five tricks is called "nap."

The Play: The highest bidder names the trump suit and makes the first lead, which must be a trump.

The cards are played in tricks. The players must follow suit to the lead card if they can. Otherwise, there is no restriction on what they may play or lead.

The winner of each trick leads to the next trick—playing any suit—and everyone continues to follow that lead. The trick is won by the highest card.

The bidder tries to win the number of tricks she has named. All the other players combine forces against her. Play stops the moment the outcome is sure—success or defeat for the bidder. **Scoring:** When a bidder wins, she collects from each other player the same number of counters as her bid. If she is defeated, she pays this number to each player.

The bid of "nap" for all the tricks is special. If you make it, you collect 10 counters from each player, but if you fail, you pay five to each one.

Loo

Players: 5 to 8 (6 is best)
Cards: A regular pack of 52
Equipment: A handful of counters—poker chips, matchsticks, toothpicks, dried beans, etc
The Deal: Each player receives three cards, one at a time. An extra hand of three cards is dealt just to the left of the dealer. This is the widow. If the player to the left of the widow does not like her hand, she may throw it away and take the widow instead. If she is satisfied with her hand, though, she must say so and stick with it.

Then each player in turn has a chance to take the widow, until somebody takes it or all refuse it.

Give the same number of counters to each player.

The Play (Single Pool): After the matter of the widow is settled, the player to the left of the dealer makes the opening lead. You must always follow suit to the lead when you can; you must play higher than any other card in the trick, if you can. Later, once trump is declared and a plain suit is led of which you have none, you must trump, if you can.

The highest trump, or, if there is no trump, the highest card of the suit led, wins the trick. Aces are high.

You must keep the tricks you have won face up on the table in front of you as you play.

Trumps: The play begins without any trump suit and continues that way so long as everybody follows suit to every lead. When somebody fails to follow suit, the top card of the undealt stock is turned over. This card decides the trump suit. The trick just played is examined and if a card that has been played turns out to be trump, that card wins the trick.

Scoring: To start a pool, the dealer must *ante up* three counters. When the pool contains no more than these three counters, it is a *single*, and play takes place as described above. After the play, the pool pays out one counter for each trick won. Players who have not won a trick must pay three counters into the next pool, making it a *double*—or jackpot.

Double Pool: This is formed by the dealer's ante of three plus any payments for *loo* (not winning a trick in the previous hand). After the deal, the next card of the deck is turned up, deciding the trump suit. After checking out their hands, the players must say in turn whether they will play or drop out. If all but the dealer drop out, he takes the pool. If only one player ahead of the dealer decides to play, the dealer must play, too. He may play for himself—in which case he cannot take the widow—or he may play to *defend the pool*, in which case he must throw away his hand and take the widow. When the dealer plays merely to defend the pool, he neither collects nor pays any counters; the pool settles with his opponent alone.

The nearest active player to the left of the dealer leads first. The other rules of play are the same as in a single pool.

The double pool pays out one-third of its contents for each trick won. A player who stays in and does not win a trick must pay three counters to the next pool.

To Win the Game: Win the largest number of counters.

Rams

Players: 3 to 5

Cards: A pack of 32. Discard all twos to sixes from a regular pack of 52. The cards rank:

(Highest)   **(Lowest)**

Equipment: A handful of counters—poker chips, matchsticks, toothpicks, dried beans, etc.

The Deal: Each player receives five cards in batches of three and two. An extra hand or *widow* is dealt, as in *Loo*. The last card belonging to the dealer is exposed to determine the trump suit.

Give the same number of counters to each player.

Declaring: After looking at their hands, the players in turn must declare whether they will play or drop out. If they play, they must undertake to win at least one trick. Any player in turn may discard the hand and take the widow instead (if it has not yet been taken).

Any player may declare *rams*—undertake to win *all* the tricks. This declaration may be made either before or after taking the widow, but it must be made before the next player has declared. In a rams game, everybody must play; players who have dropped out must pick up their hands again. If the rams player has not taken the widow, each player who has not refused it gets a chance to take it.

The Play: The player who declared rams makes the opening lead. Otherwise, it is made by the first player to the left of the dealer.

You must follow suit when you can, and you must play higher than any previous card in the trick, when you can. If a plain suit is led, you have to trump if you are able to, even if the trick has already been trumped. You must trump higher if you can. A trick is won by the highest trump in it, or, if no trump, by the highest card of the suit led.

Scoring: The dealer antes up five counters. The pool may contain counters left from the previous deal.

Each player who has stayed in the game takes one counter (or one-fifth of all the counters) from the pool for each trick he wins. Players who win no tricks must pay five counters into the next pool (as in *Loo*).

In a rams, however, the settlement is different. If the rams player wins all the tricks, she wins the whole pool plus five counters from every other player. If she loses a trick, the cards are at once thrown in: she must pay enough counters to double the pool and five counters to every player.

If everybody ahead of the player to the right of the dealer passes, this player must pay the dealer five counters if he wishes to drop. In this case, the pool remains undivided. If only one player other than the dealer decides to play, the dealer must play to defend the pool. In this case, he takes the trump card and discards another face down.

Sixty-Six

Players: 2
Cards: 24 cards: ace, king, queen, jack, ten, and nine
of each suit (Discard all twos to eights)
The Deal: Each player receives six cards, dealt three at a time. Place the rest of the pack face down in the middle of the table, to form the stock. Turn the top card of the stock face up and place it partly underneath the stock. This is the *trump* card and it decides the trump suit.
The Rank: The cards in each suit rank:

(Highest)  (Lowest)

Early Play: The non-dealer leads first. The cards are played out in tricks. A trick is won by the higher trump or by the higher card played of the suit led. The winner of a trick draws the top card of the stock, and the opponent draws the next card. In this way, each hand is restored to six cards after each trick.

During this early play, you do not have to follow suit to the lead. You may play any card. The early play ends when the stock is exhausted.
To Win the Game: You try to *meld marriages* (see below), win cards in tricks, and win the last trick. The first player to reach a total of 66 or more points wins a game point. The first one to score seven *game points* wins an overall game.
Marriages: A marriage is meld of a king and queen of the same suit. In the trump suit, a marriage counts 40. In any other

suit, it counts 20. To score a marriage, you must show it after winning a trick, then lead one of the two cards.

If the non-dealer wants to lead a king or queen from a marriage for an opening lead, she may show the marriage and then do so. But she may not score the marriage until after she has won a trick.

Trump Card: A player who has the nine of trumps may exchange it for a trump card—to get a higher trump. He may make this exchange only after winning a trick, before making the next lead.

Closing: At any turn to lead, a player may turn the trump card face down. By doing that he closes—that is, stops—any further drawing from the stock. The hands are played out as in *Later Play* (see below), except that marriages may still be melded.

Later Play: After the stock is exhausted, you play out the six cards in each hand. In this part of the game, you must follow suit to the lead, if you can.

Counting Cards: Cards won in tricks are counted as follows:

Each ace	11
Each 10	10
Each king	4
Each queen	3
Each jack	2
For winning the last trick	10

Scoring: Marriages are scored on paper whenever melded. Points taken in tricks are not entered on paper until a hand is finished, but it is important to keep mental track of these points and your opponent's points as they are won. In your turn to play, you may claim that you have reached 66. Then stop play at once and count. If you're right:

>you score one game point
>or two if your opponent has less than 33
>or three game points if he has not even won a trick.

If you are wrong, and you don't have 66:

>your opponent scores two game points.

The reason it's so important to realize when you have won a game—and to claim it—is that you may lose by playing out the hand. If you and your opponent both get more than 66, or if you tie at 65, neither of you wins. But the winner of the next hand gets one additional game point.

Usually, at least one game point is won by somebody in each deal. As mentioned earlier, you win by scoring seven game points in an overall game.

Three-Hand Sixty-Six

Players: 3
Cards: Same as in *Sixty-Six:* 24 cards, ace down to 9
The Deal: The dealer gives six cards to the other two players, but deals none to himself.
The Play: The non-dealers play regular *Sixty-Six*.
Scoring: The dealer scores the same number of game points as the winner of the deal. If both players get 66 or more—or tie at 65 (without a claim)—they score nothing and the dealer scores one. But a player is not allowed to win the overall game (seven

points) when he is the dealer. If the usual scoring would put him up to seven points or over, his total becomes six, and he must win that last point as an active player.

Four-Hand Sixty-Six

Players: 4

Cards: 32 cards from a regular pack. Ace, king, queen, jack, ten, nine, eight, and seven of each suit. (Discard twos through sixes.)

The Deal: Each player receives eight cards. The last card, turned face up for trump, is shown to each player, and then taken into the dealer's hand.

The Play: Players sitting opposite each other are partners. There is no melding. At all times you must follow suit to a lead, if possible, and also must, if possible, play higher than any card already played to the trick. When a plain suit is led and you have none, you must trump or overtrump if you can.

Scoring: Play out every hand. There is no advantage in claiming to have won. The winning side scores:

1 game point for having taken 66 to 99 or

2 game points for 100 to 129 or

3 game points for every trick (130).

If the sides tie at 65, one extra game point goes to the side winning the next hand.

WHIST GAMES

The fact is that the rules of *Whist* are simple and few. You can learn them in two minutes. *Whist* is just about the simplest of all card games to play. What is not so easy is to play *Whist* well, for its extraordinary scope for skillful play lets the expert pull miles ahead of the beginner.

Whist

Players: 4, in partnerships
Cards: Each receives 13 cards, dealt one at a time.
The Deal: The last card of the pack, belonging to the dealer, is exposed to all the players. This card decides the trump suit for that hand.
The Rank: In every suit the cards rank:

(Highest) 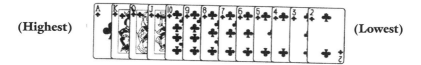 **(Lowest)**

The Play: The player to the left of the dealer makes the first lead. The hands are played out in tricks. You must follow suit to the lead if possible. Otherwise, you may play or lead as you please. However, if a player *revokes* by not following suit when he has in his hand an appropriate card to play, he and his partner have to pay a penalty. The penalty is decided upon before play begins, and may be as severe as two game points for the opponent. The partnership cannot win any trick in which it revokes.

A trick is won by the highest trump in it, or, if it contains no trump, by the highest card of the suit led. The winner of a trick makes the lead for the next trick.

One member of each partnership gathers together all the tricks won by his side. He doesn't throw them together in a single pile but overlaps them crosswise, so that each batch of four cards remains separate from the others.

To Win the Game: Win as many tricks as possible. Points for tricks and honors are accumulated, and the first side to reach a total of seven game points wins.

Scoring: The side that wins the majority of the tricks scores

> 1 game point for each trick over 6, and if agreed upon,
> 2 game points on the occasions when the opponents revoke.

In addition, points are scored for *honors*. The honors are the ace, king, queen, and jack of trumps.

> If 2 honors were dealt to each side, there is no score.
> If one side received 3 honors, it scores 2.
> For all 4 honors, the score is 4.

Remember that honors are scored by the side to which they are *dealt*, not won in play. Both sides may score in the same deal, one side winning a majority of tricks and the other side holding a majority of honors.

Dummy Whist

Players: 3
Cards: As in *Whist*
The Deal: In this adaptation of *Whist* for three players, four hands are dealt, as usual, with the extra hand or "dummy" going opposite the dealer.
The Play: The same as in *Whist*, except that the dealer plays the dummy hand as well as his own against the two live opponents. Of course, the dealer must be careful to play each hand at its proper turn.
Scoring: The dealer has a great advantage over his opponents, since he gets to see all 26 cards on his side. The fairest scoring method is to play three, six, or nine deals so that each player has the same number of turns to deal. Then the player with the highest score is declared the winner.

Bridge Whist

Players: 4, in partnerships
Cards: Same as in *Whist*
Equipment: Score pad and pencil
This game is played in the same way as basic *Whist*, but it has a number of complications.
Trumps: No trump card is turned. The dealer may name trump, if he wishes, or he may pass. If he does pass, his partner must name the trump. Any of the four suits may be named trump, or the player may call "No trump," meaning that the hand will be played without a trump suit.
Doubles: After the trump—or no trump—is named, either

one of the non-dealers may declare "I double." This multiplies the score of the winners by two.

After such a double, either member of the dealer's side may declare "I redouble" or "I double back." The teams may redouble alternately without limit, until one team quits. Then the cards are played.

The Play: After the opening lead by the player to the left of the dealer, the dealer's partner puts her cards face up on the table in vertical rows by suit. The dealer then plays the "dummy" as well as his own hand, just as in *Dummy Whist*.

Scoring: The score is kept on a score pad. The sheet is divided into two halves by a vertical line. All the scores for one team (WE) are entered in the left-hand column, and the scores of the other team (THEY) in the right. The sheet is also divided by a horizontal line, somewhat below the middle. Only odd trick scores are entered below the line, and they are accumulated to determine when a game has been won (total score of 30).

All other scores go above the line. When the play ends, each column is added up to determine the grand total won by each side, for odd tricks, honors, slams, rubbers. For instance, the score sheet may look like the illustration on the following page.

Scoring Tricks: The team winning at least six of the 13 tricks has a "book." It will score only tricks in excess of books of six. These score-able tricks are called *odd tricks*. Score them as follows:

> If trumps were s c f j No trump
> Each odd trick would count 2 4 6 8 10

Each double that was made multiplies the score of the winners by two, each redouble by four.

	WE	THEY
Honors & Bonuses	40 20 100	
Tricks		
Game 1	30	24
Game 2	120	
=		
A rubber		

Scoring Honors: Points are also scored for honors, which are written above the line on your score sheet. These are kept separate from points for tricks, which are written below the line.

The honor count is considerably more complicated than in *Whist*. When the game is played in a trump suit, the five top trumps—ace, king, queen, jack, and ten—become honors. You take the odd-trick value and multiply it by the number shown below to get the honor score, which gets written above the line.

Team with three honors or chicane	x 2
(chicane is a hand without a trump)	
Four honors divided between partners	x 4
Four honors in one hand	x 8
Four honors in one hand, fifth in partner's	x 9
Five honors in one hand	x 10

When you multiply this out, remember that the score you get is for honors only. It does not affect the scoring of the odd tricks, which you have already written below the line.

In a no-trump game, the honors are the four aces. Score them as follows:

Team with three aces	30
Four aces, divided	40
Four aces in one hand	100

Scoring Bonuses: If one side wins all 13 tricks, it scores a bonus of 40 for *grand slam*. For winning 12 tricks, a *little slam*, there is a bonus of 20. These numbers get written above the line on your score pad.

To Win the Game: The first team to win 30 points in odd tricks wins a game. The team to win a *rubber*—two games—wins a bonus of 100 points, and *the* game.

NULLO GAMES

In order to win *Nullo* games, you need to *avoid* winning tricks, or avoid taking certain cards in tricks. Most of the games are especially easy for children to learn because they have practically no other rules. Only in *Omnibus Hearts* do we find the added wrinkle that you *do* want to win some cards while you *don't* want to win others.

Four Jacks

Other Names: Polignac

Players: 4, 5, or 6

Cards: With 4 players, 32 cards as follows: ace, king, queen, jack, ten, nine, eight, seven—a full deck, but with all twos to sixes discarded. All the 32 cards are dealt; each player receives eight cards. With 5 or 6 players, 30 cards—same as above but the two black sevens are also discarded. Each player receives six or five cards.

Equipment: A handful of counters—poker chips, matchsticks, toothpicks, dried beans, etc. Distribute the same number to each player.

The Play: The player to the left of the dealer leads first. The hands are played out in tricks. There is no trump suit. Each trick is won by the highest card played by the suit led.

To Win the Game: Avoid winning any jacks. But before the opening lead, any player may announce that he will try to win all the tricks. This is called *capot*.

Scoring: Payments for holding jacks and winning capot are made into a common pool, which is divided equally among all the players when the game ends. Whenever one player is down to his last counter, all players take equal numbers of counters from the pool.

If capot is announced and made, every other player must pay five counters. But if the capot player fails to win all the tricks, he alone pays five counters.

When capot is not announced, the player who takes the jack of spades—called *Polignac*—must pay two counters into the pool. One counter must be paid for each of the other three jacks taken in.

Slobberhannes

This game is played in much the same way as *Four Jacks*, with the difference that what you want to avoid winning are:

first trick

last trick

the queen of clubs

Each of these costs one counter, and if you unluckily take all three, you must pay an extra counter—four in all.

HEARTS GAMES

This is the chief group of *Nullo* games. In all of them, the way to win is to avoid winning hearts.

If you are invited to play *Hearts* with a group that you have never played with before, it's a good idea to ask them to state the rules. Otherwise, you may find yourself playing one game while they play another.

The name of the basic game, "Hearts" is used loosely for all its offspring, but there are many variations. *Black Maria* and *Black Lady* often denote games that are different from either the *Black Lady* or *Hearts* described here.

Hearts

This is the basic and most simple game of the *Hearts* family, though the most popular is *Black Lady*.

Players: **2 to 6, but almost always 4. Other forms of the game are preferred with more or less than 4.**

Cards: **Each player receives 13 cards. When you can't divide the cards equally, remove enough deuces from the deck to make the deal come out even. Aces rank highest.**

Equipment: **A handful of counters—poker chips, matchsticks, toothpicks, dried beans, etc.—the same amount to each player—or pencil and paper.**

The Play: The player to the left of the dealer makes an opening lead and the cards are played in tricks. A trick is won by the highest card played of the suit led. There is no trump suit, though hearts are often mistakenly called "trumps." The winner of a trick leads to the next trick.

To Win the Game: Avoid winning any hearts—or win all 13 of them.

Scoring the counters: For each heart that a player wins, he must pay one counter into the pool.

If two or more players took no hearts, they divide the pool.

But if all players took hearts, nobody wins the pool. It stays on the table as a *jackpot* and becomes part of the pool for the next deal.

Scoring with pencil and paper: Each heart taken counts one point against the player. A game can be ended at any agreed-upon time, and the player with the lowest total score is the winner. The usual method is to charge a player 13 if he wins all the hearts. A good alternative is to deduct 13 (or 26, as agreed) from his score, preserving the principle that a player with a bad hand should have a chance to save himself (or gain) by taking *all* the hearts.

Heartsette

This game adapts *Hearts* to an odd number of players.

Players: 3 or 5

Cards: Place a widow (a group of cards) on the table—4 cards if three are playing, 2 cards if five are playing.

The Deal: Deal out the rest of the cards.

The Play: Play in the same way as *Hearts*, but the widow is turned face up after the first trick and goes to the winner of that trick. He must of course pay for any hearts it contains.

Spot Hearts

This variation features a different scoring method that you can apply to any member of the *Hearts* family. The charges for taking hearts go according to rank:

Ace counts	14
King counts	13
Queen counts	12
Jack counts	11
Others count	face value

Draw Hearts

This is *Hearts* for two players.

Players: 2
Cards: 13 to each player
The Deal: Place the rest of the deck face down in the middle of the table, forming the stock.
The Play: The cards are played in tricks. The winner of a trick draws the top card of the stock, and his opponent takes the next. After the stock is exhausted, the hands are played out without drawing.
To Win the Game: Take fewer hearts.

Auction Hearts

The idea of this game is to let the players bid for the privilege of naming the suit to be avoided.

Each player in turn has one chance to bid, and the highest bidder names the *minus* suit.

Bids are made in numbers of counters that the player is willing to pay into the pool. Settlement is also made with counters, as in basic *Hearts*.

If the pool becomes a jackpot, there is no bidding in the next deal. The same player retains the right to name the minus suit, without further payment, until the jackpot is won. This player also makes the opening lead.

Black Lady

This is the best-known game of the *Hearts* family. It is what
most people refer to when they speak of *Hearts*.

**Players: 3 to 7. It is best for 4, without partner
ships.**

**Cards: Deal out the whole pack, giving equal hands
to all.**

With 4 players it works out correctly.

With 3 players, discard one deuce.

With 5 players, discard two deuces.

With 6 players, discard four deuces.

With 7 players, discard three deuces.

**Equipment: A handful of counters—poker chips,
matchsticks, toothpicks, dried beans,
etc.—the same amount to each player—
or pencil and paper for scoring.**

The Pass: After looking at his hand, each player passes any
three cards he chooses to the player to his left. He must choose
which cards he is going to pass and put them on the table
before picking up the three cards passed to him by the player to
his right.

The Play: The player to the left of the dealer makes the opening lead. The cards are played out in tricks. Aces rank highest.
A trick is won by the highest card played of the suit led. The
winner of a trick leads to the next trick.

To Win the Game: Avoid taking the queen of spades—called
Black Lady, Black Maria, Calamity Jane, etc.—and avoid taking
hearts; or else take *all* the hearts *and* the queen of spades,
which is called *shooting the moon*.

Scoring: If one player takes all 14 minus cards, he can subtract

26 points from his score. Some people play instead that 26 points are added to everyone else's score. Otherwise, one point is charged for each heart won, and 13 points for the queen of spades. A running total score is kept for each player on paper. The first one to reach 100 or more loses the game, and the one with the lowest total at that time wins.

When playing with young children, you may want a shorter game. In this case, set the limit at 50.

An alternative method is to score with counters, settling after each hand. Payments are made into a pool, distributed equally to the players from time to time.

Strategy: See *Omnibus Hearts* (page 336).

Cancellation Hearts

This is a variation for 6 or more players.

Players: 6 or more

Cards: 2 packs shuffled together

The Deal: Deal the cards as far as they will go evenly. Put the extra cards face down on the table as a widow. This group of cards goes to the winner of the first trick.

The Play: You play the game exactly the same way as *Black Lady*, except:

1. When two identical cards, such as two aces of diamonds, are played in the same trick, they cancel each other out, ranking as zero. They cannot win the trick. As a result, if a deuce is led and all the higher cards of the suit played to a trick are paired and therefore canceled, the deuce would win the trick!

2. When all cards of the suit led are canceled, the cards stay on

the table and go to the next winner of a trick. The same leader leads again.

Scoring: As in *Black Lady*. Counters make for easier scoring than paper and pencil.

Discard Hearts

This is *Black Lady*, except that the three cards are sometimes passed to the left and sometimes to the right. The best plan is to alternate. The pass often allows you to ruin your neighbor. Alternate passing gives her the chance to get back at you.

Omnibus Hearts

Many players regard this as the most interesting game of the *Hearts* family. It is the same as *Black Lady* with one addition. The jack of diamonds, or sometimes the ten, is a *plus* card, counting 10 *for* you if you win it.

As a result, in this game, each suit has its own character: clubs are neutral, diamonds contain the plus card, spades contain the worst minus card, and all the hearts are minus cards. A player who makes a *take-all* must win all 13 hearts, the queen of spades, and the jack of diamonds.

Strategy: The most dangerous cards to hold are high spades— ace, king, queen—without enough lower cards to guard them. Pass such high spades when you are dealt less than three lower spades. Pass high hearts if you can afford to, and if they look dangerous, but two *low* hearts are usually enough to guard them. Any suit outside of spades is dangerous if you have four or more without any card lower than, say, a six. Even a single very low card—a two or a three—may not be a sufficient guard. Pass one to three cards from the top or middle of such a suit, if you do not have more pressing troubles.

If you do not have any high spades after the pass, lead spades at every opportunity. You can never gather Black Maria by a lower spade lead! You want to try to force her out by spade leads so that you can save yourself from winning her by discard. If you have her yourself, it is usually best to lead your shortest side suit so as to get rid of it and get the chance to discard Black Maria.

If you are dealt the jack of diamonds, pass it if you can afford to. The jack is much easier to *catch* than to save. It is not often caught by higher diamonds—and when it is, it is mostly by accident. It usually falls to the winner of the last trick. The hand with which you may hope to catch it has some aces and kings, adequately guarded by lower cards, in two or more suits. Of course, if you hope to catch the jack, don't pass any higher diamonds, and don't ever lead diamonds if you can avoid it. But put a high diamond on any diamond lead that might be won by the jack if you were to play low.

Don't attempt a take-all without a very powerful hand. Certain holdings are fatal no matter how strong you are in other suits—low hearts, for example (not at the end of a long solid suit), and the jack of diamonds (without enough diamond length and strength to save the jack even if you do not go for take-all). However, if you've got one or two middling-high hearts, it is not fatal. You may be able to win the tricks simply by leading these hearts. The players holding higher hearts may shrink from taking the tricks.

When your chief ambition is to avoid taking minus cards, which is most of the time, get rid of your high cards early rather than late. Thus, if you have:

put the ace on the *first* club lead and the jack on the *second*, saving your two to escape having to win the more dangerous third lead. The more often a suit is led, the more likely it becomes that Black Maria or hearts will be discarded on it.

WHAT THE TERMS MEAN

Around the Corner: A phrase used to describe sequences, or runs, built around the corner, such as queen, king, ace, deuce (2), 3, 4, 5, 6, 7, 8, 9, 10, and jack.

Ante, or ante up: To place a certain amount of money or counters on the table as a declaration of interest in playing the upcoming hand. In some games, only the dealer antes; in other games, all players ante.

Base cards: In solitaire, scoring cards, usually but not always aces, which are built up to complete a set, usually a full 13-card suite.

Bidding: Stating what you are willing to pay or predicting the number of tricks you hope to win.

Book: The basic number of tricks bid. In *Whist*, the first six tricks won. In *Authors*, four cards of the same rank.

Capot: Trying to win all the tricks.

Chicane: A hand without a trump card in it.

Denomination: The rank of a card, such as 2, 3, 4, etc.

Deuce: A two of any suit. "Deuce" and "two" are interchangeable terms.

Dummy: A hand that is not played by the person to whom it was dealt. Such a hand is played by that person's partner.

Face Card: A jack, queen, or king.

Follow Suit: Playing a card of the same suit that led the trick.

Gin: To lay down your whole melded hand, face up, ending the play.

Honor card: Ace, king, queen, jack of trumps, or sometimes the 10.

Knock: To lay down all melds and declare the face value of unmelded cards.

Lead: The first play that establishes the suit to follow.

Marriage: A meld of king and queen in the same suit.

Meld: Any scoring combination of cards announced, shown, or played; it refers to combinations of three of a kind and/or three or more cards in sequence.

Nullo games: Games in which you avoid taking certain cards.

Picture card: Jack, queen, or king.

Pip Value: The counting value of a card. For example, in most games the counting value of 3 is 3, etc. In *Black Jack*, however, an ace has a counting value of 1 or 11.

Renege: To fail to follow suit when able to do so.

Revoke: To fail to play as required by the rules of the game. A revoke can mean the same thing as a renege (not following suit when you could have and were supposed to), but it usually has a broader meaning and covers the violation of any rule of the game.

Spot card: Any card from 2 to 10.

Suits: There are four: hearts, diamonds, clubs, and spades.

Sweep: Generally means winning/taking every trick in a hand of play. In *Cassino*, a sweep is taking all the cards on the table in one play.

Tricks: The cards taken/won in one round of play.

Trump suit: The suit that can overtake the others and win over the cards of the other suits. For example, if the trump suit is diamonds, any diamond can win over any card of any other suit. Each game has its own process for selecting a trump suit.

Upcard: The top card of the stock, turned over beside the stockpile, which starts the discard pile.

Widow: A group of cards dealt separately in their own pile apart from the players' hands. In some games, such as *Hearts*, the widow consists of the undealt portion of the deck and is taken by the winner of the first trick.

Wild cards: Cards that, prior to the game, may be given any value you choose.

CARD TRICK CHART AND INDEX

CARD GAME CHART AND INDEX